THE
Imperfect
LEADER

A STORY ABOUT DISCOVERING THE *NOT-SO-SECRET*
SECRETS OF TRANSFORMATIONAL LEADERSHIP

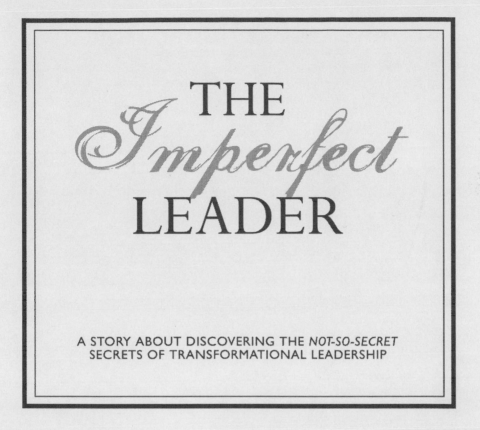

BY

DAVIS H. TAYLOR

authorHOUSE®

AuthorHouse™
1663 Liberty Drive, Suite 200
Bloomington, IN 47403
www.authorhouse.com
Phone: 1-800-839-8640

First published by AuthorHouse   8/21/2007

ISBN: 978-1-4343-2084-1 (sc)
ISBN: 978-1-4343-2085-8 (hc)

Library of Congress Control Number: 2007904692

Printed in the United States of America
Bloomington, Indiana

This book is printed on acid-free paper.

Dedicated to Denise... love of my life,
soul mate, and partner in the journey.

PREFACE

I wrote *The Imperfect Leader* to explore the *not-so-secret* secrets of transformational leadership. *Not-so-secret* because the leadership model espoused herein has been proven through the centuries to have a positive, lasting impact on the world, and because many readers will recognize as truth the ideas presented. *Secret* because these truths run counter to many prevailing leadership practices. While readers may acknowledge and accept the ideas offered, acceptance is one thing— embracing them and living them is another matter altogether.

Ultimately, my purpose in writing is to spark awareness of and conversation around the ideas presented about leadership—the kind of leadership that can make a difference in the world.

During my school years and throughout my career I experienced many types of leaders in various walks of life. No doubt you had similar experiences. Observing or working for numerous leaders, I realized a few were great, some were good, but the vast majority either did not understand the essence of transformational leadership or chose not to embrace it. If I am brutally honest about my own effectiveness as a leader, I must admit that all too often my leadership was far from transformational. This realization—recognizing my own imperfection—set me on a journey to search, to learn, and to grow.

I have discovered it takes a certain kind of leader to drive transformational change—it takes a leader who embraces a worthy mission, envisions a compelling preferred future, and then leads from personally held core values to engage and motivate employees to exceptional performance. I also began to understand that while leadership may be more art than science, there is a proven leadership model that outperforms all others, a philosophy that predictably delivers extraordinary and sustainable results.

The Imperfect Leader is an attempt to articulate these truths; however, it is not a story about me; it is a work of fiction. I hope readers will identify with the circumstances and challenges faced by this story's characters. Each was pulled together from a lifetime of watching leaders in action; any resemblance to specific people is purely coincidental. With a few notable exceptions, the same is true for any company mentioned in the story.

My fervent hope is that you—leaders at every level and in all walks of life—will recognize certain aspects of yourselves within these pages and will accept the necessity for—and challenge to—personal transformation. My dream is that you will embrace and recognize the inherent power of these truths and as a result, you will become a vital force in transforming your organization—and in transforming society as a whole.

Davis H. Taylor

ONE

" Life shrinks or expands in
proportion to one's courage. "

ANAIS NIN

"Get the hell out of my office before I throw you out!"

Trembling with rage, Josh immediately regretted his words to
the CFO, despite the fact he felt justified in his anger. He knew the
situation had been coming to a head for some time.

Almost two years earlier, when he first joined National Service
Masters, Josh was elated about his admission to the "inner circle," as
the new executive vice president for operations. The position was a
perfect fit: creating strategy, building teams, motivating the workforce,
delivering results—in fact, the only imperfection about the job was his
relationship with other members of the executive team.

1

In effect, the problem was a matter of leadership philosophy. On one hand, Josh valued his people, taking great care to provide direction, while training, motivating, encouraging, and building trust. On the other hand, he routinely found himself disagreeing with other executive-team members who openly disdained the blue-collar workforce and seemingly made decisions based on their personal ambitions and the impact on short-term stock price.

The situation came to a head during a tense discussion with the CFO over headcount reductions. Pressing his demand, the CFO said, "Listen, I don't care what you think, I want your plan for a ten percent reduction-in-force on my desk by tomorrow." Appalled by the damage another round of headcount reductions would do to employee morale, not to mention the negative impact it would have on recently launched growth strategies, Josh was so furious he ordered the CFO out of his office.

While Josh wasn't surprised that Matthew Richardson, the CEO, would learn of the altercation with the CFO, he wasn't prepared for the message Matt was about to deliver. "Josh," he began, "I trust you more than anyone on my team. You're a talented, strategic thinker, and you probably work harder than anyone at National. The people in the field respect you and will follow you anywhere. But, Josh, there is a problem… you just don't fit with our executive team. If you submit your resignation by Monday, we'll arrange to give you nine months severance pay."

So began the descent.

Josh's midday walk around the small community lake varied little from those of preceding days and weeks. It had been a hot, dry summer, and Josh, too, felt dried-up and useless. Thinking out loud, almost frantically, he whispered, "How did it get to this? Am I totally ineffective? What's wrong with me?"

The descent had been hard.

At first, Josh's involuntary separation from National seemed like a blessing. Armed with extensive contacts in the investment community, a bull market, and a plan to buy several synergistic training and consulting companies, he set out to build a leadership development company that could make a difference in the workplace. The plan was solid, and Josh had no trouble attracting acquisition target companies interested in the opportunity.

As luck would have it, in a matter of weeks the investment environment dramatically changed as the dot.com bubble burst. Seemingly overnight, billions of dollars were lost in company valuations. Potential investors got "cold feet," and Josh was left with a solid business plan but no funding sources.

Josh was undeterred. Filled with self-confidence—and what he believed to be the necessary ability—Josh embarked to build from scratch his own leadership-consulting practice.

In short order, he signed as clients several small companies that could benefit from his leadership experience and business acumen. It appeared the consulting practice was off to a promising start.

Although working diligently to serve his clients, Josh soon encountered the perfect storm into which many solo-practitioner consultants sail: lack of clear market differentiation, inadequate business development efforts, and, consequently, insufficient cash flow. Compounding Josh's discomfort in the new endeavor was the very fact that he was operating solo. Previously, he had spent more than twenty years building teams and leading groups of people in large enterprises— he did not enjoy working alone. Soon it became apparent his small client base was insufficient to adequately finance the tiny firm.

Accepting reality, Josh explained to his wife, Libby, "This consulting thing isn't working." He intended to reenter the corporate arena.

That conversation with Libby was almost a year ago. Since then he'd found job leads sparse, and the interviews he had been able to secure simply hadn't gone well. His once seemingly strong contact list was totally ineffective, and his network unresponsive. He and Libby sold their house to make ends meet and moved to rental property with their four children. Money set aside for the kids' education was consumed by living expenses. They even dug into their 401k to pay the rent and buy groceries. Seeking income and health benefits, Libby returned to the workforce in a clerical job.

Days of unemployment turned into weeks, and then months. Josh was discouraged, damaged, and depressed. Cash was running low. He couldn't find work he enjoyed—or any work at all, for that matter. He reflected on his inability to secure employment; his failure to provide for his family; his inability to find personal significance. Wouldn't it be better if he simply "checked out"?

The descent was complete.

Walking around the lake, Josh felt alone and hopeless. In despair, he collapsed at the foot of a large oak, tears flowing from his eyes. Unable to gather inner-courage to go on, in desperation he cried, "Please, God...."

At the base of the tree, unaware of passing time, Josh sat motionless, lost in a private world of self-pity—until a voice interrupted his thoughts.

"Excuse me young man, I don't want to intrude. Are you all right?"

Josh looked up to see an older gentleman standing beside him. Gradually he realized the man was one with whom he had exchanged greetings during his daily walks. They had never stopped to talk—in fact, Josh had intentionally avoided conversation with the man who now knelt beside him. Embarrassed, Josh jumped to his feet, and wiped the tears from his eyes. "No…uh, thanks…I mean, uh, yes…I'm fine," he muttered.

"Another hot one," the man offered, "we certainly could use some rain."

"Yes," Josh said, "I mean…yes, it is hot. Too hot. Guess I just needed to take a break…listen, thanks for your concern. I probably need to get going."

"Fine," the man replied, "I certainly didn't want to intrude. I apologize for the interruption; I had no right to impose on you."

"No, it's not that. You're not imposing. I simply needed to take a break…I just lost track of time."

"You know," the man said, "they say time is the great healer."

The words tore at Josh and he fought to control the tears. How urgently he craved escape from feelings of inadequacy, humiliation, and embarrassment. How desperately he craved healing for his injured pride.

The man escorted Josh to the path that circled the lake. "Undoubtedly you have family and friends in whom you confide," he began, "but, in their absence I'd be glad to listen, if you want to talk."

"It's complicated," Josh said. "I really don't know where to begin. It's just that I'm in transition and things don't seem to be working out too well. It's complicated," he repeated.

"Why not put aside the complicated part, and start with something easy," the man said.

"Like what?"

"Well, perhaps we should start with the formalities." The man grinned as he extended his hand to Josh. "My name is George Greenfield."

Awkwardly, Josh took the man's hand. "Pleasure to meet you, Mr. Greenfield. I'm Josh McCall."

"Please, call me George. McCall…is that a Scottish name?"

"Yes," Josh replied, "but I've never taken time to investigate my heritage beyond that basic fact…guess I don't know the whole story."

"You might want to do that some day. It might be that you discover some very interesting stories. You know, Josh, our stories are important. They give us clues as to who we are, where we've been and where we're going. What is your story, Josh?"

Our stories are important. They give us clues as to who we are, where we've been and where we're going.

"What do you mean by 'my story'?"

"Why not begin by telling me about yourself?" George suggested.

TWO

Joshua David McCall was born in Heidelberg, Germany, into the home of a career U.S. Army officer. His early years were marked by the family's numerous change-of-station assignments to various military posts in the States and abroad.

When Josh was fifteen his father retired from the army and moved to Washington, D.C. There Josh entered high school and found himself attracted to student government. Each year he was elected a class officer, and each year his confidence grew. Achievement and personal recognition motivated Josh, that is, until he experienced a humiliating defeat while running for student body president.

Lacking the self-awareness to recognize his personal traits that tended toward arrogance and self-absorption, and missing valuable lessons from the experience, Josh abandoned student government activities and distanced himself from his classmates. Josh graduated high school unfocused and unfulfilled—and, ironically, void of personal achievement and recognition.

Next he enrolled at a military college in the Southeast, a logical choice given his father's military career. The discipline and structured environment were good for Josh and were important determinants in his ability to, at least minimally, attend to academic requirements. Structure and discipline aside, Josh's college years were unexceptional and he graduated undistinguished in any way whatsoever.

Upon graduation, Josh was commissioned as an army officer, and subsequent years found him at various duty stations in the United States and overseas. During a thirty-day furlough at his parents' home in Washington, D.C., he met and proposed to Elizabeth (Libby) Whitman, who soon thereafter became his wife.

Military life suited Josh well; rebounding from lackluster academic days, he performed in an exemplary manner in both line and staff roles. While his strong preference was for leadership roles in line units, unfortunately he received several consecutive assignments with staff responsibility at the headquarters level. Driven by restlessness, ambition, and not a little pride, Josh was disillusioned—he decided to resign from the military in favor of civilian pursuits, which would allow advancement based on individual capabilities, professional performance, and personal preferences.

Josh's decision to leave the military eventually led to a sales job for ChemExperts, a national distributor of industrial chemical products. His first year at ChemExperts was remarkable. Josh had the good fortune of inheriting a neglected sales territory, vacated by a less-than-diligent predecessor. During this time, Libby gave birth to Matthew David McCall.

Within weeks of Matthew's birth, ChemExperts promoted Josh. His task was to turn around the company's most under-performing sales region. While the timing was less than ideal, Josh was eager to advance his career and disinclined to forego a prized promotion into management.

At the time of Josh's arrival, the ChemExperts' Midwest region was in dire straits. Sales lagged to the point that the region was dead last in the company's financial results. Morale was low and turnover unacceptably high, especially among field sales representatives.

After months of intense effort, Josh dramatically increased sales and managed a perfect retention rate among the sales force and customer service group. As a result of Josh's outstanding performance, the Midwest region was recognized as number-one in the country. Elated, Josh felt more than a little pride, thoroughly enjoying the public acclamation.

Libby, too, was thrilled with the honors Josh received. She encouraged him with genuine praise, and quickly added—now that Josh had accomplished the task and earned appropriate recognition— it would be good to have him home with the family more often.

Admitting he had neglected his family, Josh set a more measured, rational pace at work and greatly extended his time with Libby and Matt. Soon, Libby announced they were expecting a second addition to the McCall family.

Following closely on the heels of Libby's pronouncement, Josh was selected as the new director of corporate sales and was given the task of rejuvenating and revitalizing the company's stagnant corporate sales program.

His new responsibilities were exhilarating, involving close

interaction with his senior management as well as extensive customer meetings, entertainment, and negotiations with top corporate purchasing managers. However, his extended absences caused stress at home and left him feeling somewhat out of touch with his young sons.

Justifying to Libby his frequent absences and lack of availability, Josh insisted the travel and intense work schedule were necessary for career progression. Once he achieved the coveted promotion to vice president, things would slow down; the family would have the income it needed and Josh would be in the position to which he aspired.

Josh performed well in the new role, almost doubling sales with corporate accounts. Company executives were delighted, so much so that when a zone vice president position became available, they promoted another capable candidate to the job in order to keep Josh in the corporate sales role. Josh was infuriated: His superiors had promised a promotion and now reneged.

Again discouraged, and now acutely restless, Josh returned halfheartedly to his work, focusing instead on networking activity that could unveil opportunities in which his leadership contributions could be fully realized and appreciated.

Josh had no problem connecting with executive recruiters and soon landed with Trans Continental Foods, an importer/exporter and distributor of international food products. Lured with an attractive compensation plan and the title of vice president, Josh accepted a sales and marketing position with responsibility for the market launch of new products imported from Asia.

Trans Continental was an exciting environment for Josh, and he was quite impressed with his new boss, Randy Ackerman, an articulate, intelligent "climber" in the organization. Taking Josh under his wing, Randy initiated an informal mentoring relationship, offering to help

Josh smooth rough edges and acquire the political skills necessary to succeed in a large corporation. During frequent conversations Randy explained the fine art of positioning, the rationale for situational ethics, the need to self-promote, and the importance of a whatever-it-takes attitude to hit the numbers. While these lessons were somewhat inconsistent with his own values, Josh observed how Randy's espoused leadership principles certainly served *him* well in navigating a career in the huge company.

Over time, Josh became more politically correct, and while he never crossed an ethical line, he allowed others to invoke situational ethics without question. Josh also initiated efforts at self-promotion, or as Randy would put it, "The art of making sure you get the credit and recognition you deserve."

Josh's work kept him on the road constantly, much to Libby's chagrin, especially now that she was again pregnant, this time with twins. Assuring her things would be different, he endeavored to cut back on the travel, especially internationally.

Meanwhile the new product launch went exceedingly well and Josh's team achieved national prominence for the new brand much sooner than anyone anticipated.

One afternoon Josh anticipated the usual monthly mentoring-and-direction meeting with his boss. Instead he was stunned by Randy's announcement that, due to Josh's success, the new product line would be rolled into mainstream company distribution channels and Josh and his team would be downsized as unnecessary to company operations.

Josh felt like he had been shot. He dreaded telling Libby news of his personal defeat, especially in light of the fact the babies would be born within the month.

Fortunately, Libby took the news well, focusing on positives, like

Josh's ability to find a new job and the opportunity to find a position requiring less travel. He knew she was right, but *his* problem wasn't with the future, it was in dealing with the shame and humiliation of being fired, or downsized, or whatever the company chose to call it.

> *His problem wasn't with the future, it was in dealing with the shame and humiliation of being fired, or downsized, or whatever the company chose to call it.*

Scouring his contact file, Josh eventually connected with Sam Lazzaro, a former army boss. Now an accomplished investment banker, Sam was delighted to hear from his former protégé—he needed someone like Josh to take over as CEO for a failing start-up business.

DC Technologies had patented a unique compression technology, allowing secure transmission of digital communication packets through radio air waves. While the military apparently was interested, the previous CEO was unable to execute a successful sales-and-marketing plan. Josh readily agreed to take on the role. With much consternation Libby reluctantly agreed Josh should take the job, provided they could be sure it would work out before relocating the family. Josh agreed and spent the next twelve months commuting between his home and the company headquarters.

The year was a whirlwind of activity, with Josh's time divided equally between building an effective team at the company, taking a "road show" to potential investors, and making business-development calls on various branches of the military. Josh's efforts paid off when the navy agreed to purchase substantial interest in the technology, with the provision that the technology perform as promised during a three-month test.

Unfortunately, the technology did not perform as expected and the navy cancelled the contract. Having no alternatives, Josh entered the company into Chapter 11 bankruptcy proceedings and resigned to return home to his family in Doylestown, Pennsylvania.

THREE

Concluding with details about his experience at National Service Masters, the training company business plan, and his foray into consulting, Josh's narrative came to a close.

"Quite a story," George remarked. "Tell me, Josh, after all the jobs you held in various industries, what made you decide to pursue a consulting career?"

"Well," Josh mused, "ultimately I suppose there were two factors behind my decision: First, I have always focused on developing and motivating my people, and because I was careful to demonstrate that I cared, they've always done a good job for me. Second, too frequently my bosses were driven by political correctness, situational ethics, personal ambition, or just plain greed. They were more focused on themselves than on motivating their people to get a job done. My intent was to teach leaders how to inspire employees to get great results."

"A lofty goal," George said. "Is that still what you want to do? Is it still important to you?"

"Frankly, George, I don't know what I want to do. Nor do I know what I *ought* to do. After the false starts and roadblocks I've experienced, I'm not sure I know—with any confidence—what I'm capable of doing."

George considered Josh's words before responding: "Do you mind if I ask you a few questions?"

"Of course not," Josh answered. "Fire away."

Thoughtfully, George began: "First, Josh, what specifically are you trying to do in life? Second, what is it about *you* that is standing in the way?"

"What is it about *me* that is standing in the way?" Josh asked incredulously.

Have you ever stopped to consider why someone would want to be led by you?

"Yes," George replied, "and, what do you think you know—with absolute conviction—about your purpose in life?"

Silence.

After a pause George continued: "Finally, have you ever stopped to consider why someone would *want* to be led by you?"

Josh was stunned by the audacity of the man's questions.

FOUR

Several days passed with Josh avoiding his habitual lakeside walk. Frankly, he wasn't keen on another encounter with George and his piercing questions. Thinking back on the unpleasant occasion, Josh felt good about the way he controlled his response to the older man. He had been polite yet formal as he excused himself from the troubling discussion.

Inside, Josh seethed with anger at George's questions, thinking: *What does the old man know about me, or about leadership? I've been incredibly successful during my career! I delivered results and earned positions of increasing scope and responsibility! I'm capable. I'm focused. I know how to lead, damn it!*

Days later, the questions still haunted him. Josh mulled the verbal debate that would ensue should he and George resume the conversation. Mentally, Josh played out arguments and counter arguments, yet the more he tried to develop his line of reasoning the more anxious he became about his anticipated rejoinder. The fact was Josh didn't *feel* like an accomplished leader. He felt like a failure. Could it be that George saw something in Josh that he himself could not discern?

Partly in desperation, partly in a desire for personal redemption, Josh resolved to seek out George. Josh wanted—no, to be honest—he *needed* answers.

Thumbing through the telephone white pages Josh found an entry for George Greenfield. Picking up the phone, he tentatively dialed the number.

Momentarily a familiar voice answered the call and after an exchange of greetings George asked, "To what, may I ask, do I owe the honor of this call?"

"Mr. Greenfield…I mean, George…I was wondering if we could get together to talk?"

"Of course," George said, "I was about to leave for a stroll. Would you care to join me by the lake?"

"Sure," Josh replied, "I'd welcome the opportunity."

Josh found George standing near the lake, taking refuge from the sun under the large oak. Speaking out loud, albeit mostly to himself,

Josh remarked, "Wonder if this drought is ever going to end."

Hearing the comment, George responded, "That would be nice, everything is so dry. It's times like these that make us appreciate the rain. I suppose we never are satisfied with what we have…." George's words trailed off as if he expected Josh to speak.

The two men sat for a while in silence. Finally George asked, "What's on your mind, Josh?"

"George, last week when we met, you asked some very pointed questions. The more I think about them, the more perplexed I become. The fact is I really don't understand what you were trying to say."

"Josh, do you remember the movie *Forrest Gump?*"

"Sure," Josh said. "That was a great movie."

"Do you remember that Forrest's running ability was instrumental in placing him in a myriad of situations with prominent historical figures of the 1960s?"

"Yes," Josh replied, not at all sure where the questions were leading.

"Well, Josh, your story reminded me of Forrest Gump."

"In what way?" Josh asked.

"In many ways," George said. "Like his, your story includes interesting situations and opportunities, it involves some intriguing people, and it takes place on a global stage. While these things clearly are reminiscent of the *Gump* movie, it's actually the running part that most reminds me of you."

"Oh…" Josh said, stifling a smirk, "how so?"

"It seems to me, Josh, that you've been constantly on the run… running this way and that…running away from, or running toward, or running nowhere in particular…yet always running. I can't help but wonder, Josh. Why were you running? What were you trying to do?"

Josh replied, "I guess you could say I've been running. It's been a hectic, fast-paced career. But I wasn't running *away*. It's just that right now success doesn't have a name, it doesn't have a face, and I'm not quite sure how to get there…so I just keep charging ahead."

"Whether you are running forward or backward, it really doesn't matter," George said. "Unless you know specifically what you're trying to do, all that running just takes you in the wrong direction or around in circles."

Josh contemplated George's words. Finally he asked, "Are you suggesting I need to define success in order to give meaning to my running?"

"Actually my point is something very different. A wise man once said, 'Success is in the journey.' The statement implies success is not so much a destination, but a sense of being while one is in route to a destination. In order to achieve success, we first must have a purpose for which to live, and our purpose will be the guiding light in all we undertake. Success is merely the measure that evaluates how we arrive at our destination. Success is not, in itself, *the* destination."

Success is not so much a destination, but a sense of being while one is in route to a destination.

Josh questioned, "So you think my problem is that I've been seeking something called success instead of pursuing some unexpressed purpose?"

"Well, that's part of my point. Don't feel alone, Josh; unfortunately it's the human condition to seek success rather than purpose. As a result, literally millions of people around the globe lead lives of frantic activity at a frenzied pace and end up disillusioned, disappointed, often depressed…all the while wondering why they feel insignificant… wondering if their lives will count for anything."

"Yeah, I know the feeling all too well," Josh replied.

George continued: "For some people purpose may be difficult to articulate. It's a somewhat innate comprehension of *why* one exists. Often it's easiest to express one's purpose through combined elements that reflect the individual's purpose.

"Let me explain, beginning with the concept of mission. Our mission is the thing that drives us. It's our stated end goal for *what* we exist to accomplish. Vision is a preferred future, or what the end goal for our existence *looks* like. Values are derived from our beliefs and worldview, and are the fundamental building blocks to what we consider acceptable behavior, both for ourselves and for others. When we understand our mission, vision, and values, then we understand *what it is we are trying to do.*"

Mission is the thing that drives us. It's our stated end goal for what we exist to accomplish.

Josh thought for a moment, and then commented, "So you're suggesting that my pursuit of success may be obscuring a deeper, more significant purpose...."

"Yes," George said, "once you identify and act on that inner purpose—one that brings together every aspect of your life, connecting your values, beliefs and talents with things about which you are most passionate—then you will experience fulfillment and lead a life of significance. And, in so doing, you can experience success on a daily basis."

"Okay," Josh mused, "Suppose I agree. The other day you said there were other important questions. How do they fit in?"

Standing, George brushed dried grass from his clothes. "Can we take a walk? My circulation could use a boost."

Joining George on the path, Josh described his anger during their first encounter: "George, I was really irritated by your questions, and at the insinuation that I was the problem."

"Josh, I'm truly sorry you were offended. My goal was not to lay blame, but to challenge you to seek underlying causes for your professional difficulties. We just discussed the importance of purpose in order to learn what you're trying to do. If you are clear about your purpose, the next logical question is this: What is it about you that could be standing in the way?"

"Yeah, that was the question that really hacked me off. Look, George, I'm just like everybody else. I'm trying to make a living—trying to provide for my family. The fact is, I've done well in every job I ever had. In every situation setbacks and problems were out of my control, resulting from other people's poor judgment, or greed, or ambition, or in the case of DC Tech, faulty technologies. I've always been able to take lemons and make lemonade. I proved my value as a capable businessman. I'm a competent leader. So what do you mean, what is it about *me* that is standing in the way?"

"While it's a very personal question," acknowledged George, "one shouldn't take it too personally. Each individual should pause to answer the question at some point in life. Early in my own career I struggled due to lack of direction, and from an inability to work in teams. My problem wasn't that I couldn't work with others; it was that I had extreme confidence in my own ability. As a result, I failed to include others in decision making, which left them de-motivated and un-empowered. These troubled experiences taught me the importance of the combined influences of focus and character.

"Focus is possible when we first answer the *trying to do* question—when we articulate our mission and vision. Character reflects the *way* in which we go about what we're trying to do.

"Focus and character refer to values. If we're focused on our mission and vision, then it may be reasoned that one of our values is achieving purpose—and this purpose gives us direction. Moreover, the way we behave and the manner in which we live and work with others are indicators of our values. Ultimately, values govern behavior and behavior determines performance. If you possess clear mission and vision, yet still fail to achieve desired performance, the root cause may be an issue of personal values."

> *Values govern behavior and behavior determines performance.*

Concluding, George reiterated, "Thus the question: *What else is it about you that is standing in the way?*"

"Then on top of the *purpose thing*, you're suggesting my personal values are also out of whack?" Josh was clearly agitated.

"Not necessarily," George replied. "What I *am* suggesting is that you may have allowed outside influences to distract you, or you may have allowed them to compromise your values. Let's consider examples from your story to illustrate my point.

"First, let's establish the fact that compassion—or love—is a value. Last week you described in glowing terms your love for Libby and your children. You also talked about extended periods of travel that took you away from home and how those absences negatively impacted your family—and you told me you sometimes regretted the choices you made. The fact that you made those choices doesn't suggest that you don't value love. It does indicate, however, that you allowed another motivation or influence to compromise that value—at least in regard to your family—for a specific period of time.

"Another example is from your tenure with Trans Continental, working for that Ackerman fellow. You told me about your uneasiness with the way he embraced the concept of situational ethics. You also told me integrity is important to you. Integrity is a value. The fact that you condoned Ackerman's situational ethics doesn't mean you

21

don't value integrity. It *does* mean you conceded that value to appease Ackerman.

"In each case there were consequences for not living your values. In the case of your family, the resulting performance was a somewhat fractured family unit, at least temporarily. In the case of Ackerman's situational ethics, the performance implications were perhaps more complex. While you didn't personally behave unethically, the compromise you made to accept his behavior clearly inhibited your ability to speak out against that behavior. Additionally, it's possible observers might conclude that you, too, embraced the notion of situational ethics. Worse still, they might question your character based on the observation that you say one thing, yet condone another.

"Ultimately, character is what's inside you. It's predicated on your core values and manifested through your behavior. The only way others can ascertain your character is to observe your behavior—for better or worse. Please understand, Josh, I'm not questioning your character. I simply hope you'll understand the importance of focusing on your purpose and striving to live your values."

"That's a lot to take in," Josh said. "So, what about the third question?"

"You mean, *why would anyone want to be led by you?*"

"That's the one."

"For the most part, Josh, the question is answered once you address mission, vision, and values. Some management guru once said, 'People want and need to be led.' I would expand that thought by saying people want and need to be led by a leader who identifies and embraces a worthy mission, clearly articulates a preferred future or vision, and then models and exemplifies behavior prescribed by shared values to enable the vision and effectively execute the mission."

"That's all?" Josh asked, hardly disguising his sarcasm.

George countered, "Not quite. The rest of the answer lies in what one believes about the essence of leadership and in what type of leadership one practices."

People want and need to be led.

"Sounds pretty philosophical," Josh responded skeptically.

"Not really," George replied. "The concept is quite simple and concrete; it's the execution that's difficult, especially if one endeavors to practice the *one* approach to leadership proven to outperform all others."

Now sincerely interested, Josh asked, "And what approach is that?"

"Tell you what," George said, "next Saturday the chamber of commerce is sponsoring a lecture on the topic. Perhaps you will join me to learn more. In the meantime, a word of encouragement: No doubt you'll struggle with some of the things we talked about today. It is important to realize—as you lead at home, at work, or wherever—you *will* make mistakes. Josh, you must learn to accept the fact that no leader is perfect…it's the journey that matters."

No leader is perfect…it's the journey that matters.

Having circled the lake, the two men retired for the day.

FIVE

Later that evening Josh checked his calendar and telephoned George to confirm the Saturday appointment. Before hanging up, Josh impulsively added, "George, if you don't mind, there's something I need to know."

"Yes, go on."

"George, why are you doing this? Why are you spending so much time with me?"

"Let me tell you a story," George said.

25

• ● •

George Greenfield lived an advantaged life, having been born to an upper-middle class family in Colorado. A conscientious student, he attended an Ivy League school in the Northeast, graduated with honors, and went on to earn an MBA at a top-tier business school.

Completing his education, George was recruited for a position in the sporting goods industry, a field in which he had keen interest. There, over the course of his career, George made significant contributions in the areas of business development and operations, ascending the corporate hierarchy in various roles.

While his rise was continuous, it was not without setbacks. Early on as a team member, and later as manager, George grappled with two key issues. The first was the need to maintain focus on strategic direction. Eager to deliver performance and get results, too often he became mired in tactical execution and fell prey to tyranny of the urgent, losing sight of the bigger picture and strategic objectives. Second, he frequently was at odds with team members due to overconfidence and a conviction that *his* way was the *right* way to do things.

As his career progressed, George's take-charge, hands-on, results-oriented leadership style was widely acknowledged and appreciated, and, at a relatively young age, he was selected to take the helm of a joint venture between two prominent players in a specialty niche of the sporting goods industry.

At Extreme Ltd., George's focus was on bringing together the merged companies. Because his primary strengths were in sales and operations he realized the need to recruit outside talent to fill the void.

After a surprisingly difficult job search, George scored a coup, luring from a competitor a capable senior executive to fill the chief marketing role. Soon an accomplished marketing professional, Karen Kowalski, was on board to lead the company's global sales and marketing efforts.

Within a year, it became obvious to Karen that the new relationship was not working out as she had anticipated.

Relying on his own considerable abilities and business acumen, George unwittingly exerted undue influence and control over Karen's area of responsibility. Oblivious to the tension he was causing, George routinely micro-managed Karen's efforts, stifling her initiative and limiting her leadership of the marketing group. Finally Karen had all she could take—she resigned, leaving George to manage the floundering marketing effort he had created.

During this same timeframe, a group of young executives asked George to teach them about leadership. Meeting with the small group on a weekly basis, George discovered that the more he taught, the more he learned. And as he learned, he became increasingly aware of several things: First, he became keenly aware of the role he had played in precipitating Karen's abrupt departure from Extreme. His hands-on, results-focused approach stifled Karen's initiative and did nothing to maximize her leadership potential.

Second, George began to understand that while leadership may be more art than science, there *was* a proven leadership model that outperformed all others, a philosophy that

> *While leadership may be more art than science, there is a proven leadership model that outperforms all others.*

predictably delivers extraordinary and sustainable results.

Finally, George discovered how much he enjoyed guiding and encouraging these young leaders to new heights of leadership; it seemed the most invigorating experience of his career. Consequently, George enrolled in a doctorate program and subsequently resigned from Extreme to launch a consulting practice specializing in leadership development.

• ● •

Concluding, George said, "Ultimately, I discovered there are three traditional leadership styles. Mine was the position-based style, with the goal of delivering results through personal expertise and ability. My approach was to exercise power, with emphasis on command and control. In doing so I unwittingly suppressed my employees, creating an environment in which they avoided initiative, risk-taking, and creativity—an environment in which they could not readily grow."

"You mentioned three styles," Josh said. "What are the other two?"

"One is processed-based and the other is personality-based," George replied. "Process-based leaders are more operationally driven and tend to manage outcomes through process, policy, and procedure. Personality-based leaders maximize human resources by building strong relationships and teams."

"Which of the three leadership styles do you think is most effective?" Josh asked.

"Each leadership style is effective in specific circumstances, and each is imperfect in its own way. In reality, effectiveness is less about style and more about philosophy—it's about which leadership model one embraces."

"And what model is that?" Josh asked.

"It's actually very simple in concept," George answered, "but to gain a complete understanding, perhaps it's best to gain the full picture. This philosophy is the topic of the lecture on Saturday. Could we wait until then to explore the matter?"

"Certainly," Josh said a bit impatiently, "if you think that's best."

"One last thing," George added. "You asked why I'm spending so much time with you. Josh, you are a talented individual and I want to help in any way I can. It's important to me—it's my *calling*, so to speak—to do everything possible to help others understand the true essence of leadership."

"Thank you, George, you're very kind."

"It's my pleasure, and I look forward to future conversations. In the meantime, feel free to drop me an e-mail if there is anything you'd like to discuss. My address is: *greenfield at values dot com*."

After speaking with George, Josh told Libby of the day's events. Late that evening he composed an e-mail.

From: jdmccall@emailxpress.com
Sent: Wednesday, July 19, 2006 11:16 PM
To: greenfield@values.com
Subject: More thoughts ...

George -

First, thanks for the time you've given me to talk these past two weeks—you've provided much food for thought. Frankly, I'm anxious about some of the questions you raised and even more concerned by my responses. It's taxing to reflect on what I thought was a successful (there's that word again!) career only to realize the host of mistakes I've made. So, here's what I'm thinking...

Just as you admitted imperfections, it appears I've made some fairly major mistakes: The first was to run after what I called success, rather than trying to understand my purpose. Funny that I never thought of it that way. Success for me has always been the next promotion, the next big title, the next increased responsibility, the next bigger paycheck, the next fancier house...well you know what I mean...it's all the stuff that defines "what" I am instead of "who" I am.

The second—and bigger—mistake is compromising my values. It really stings to realize the neglect of my family, and I'm committed to changing that. Also, your comments about Ackerman really hit home, and I need to give them more thought.

An additional question: As I think through the concepts of mission, values, and vision on a personal level, I'm wondering how you see them playing out on an organizational level.

Finally, thanks for your interest and encouragement.

Josh

From: greenfield@values.com
Sent: Thursday, July 20, 2006 8:48 AM
To: jdmccall@emailxpress.com

Subject: More thoughts ...

Dear Josh,

Again, please know it's my pleasure to spend time with you and to help in any way I can. I'm delighted you found the conversation useful. It sounds to me like you're on the right track.

Your question about mission, vision, and values in an organizational scenario is quite timely—these topics will be addressed to some extent during the lecture on Saturday. If you like, you can ride with me. Unless I hear otherwise, I'll pick you up at 8:30.

Best regards,
G. Greenfield

SIX

66 You must be the change
you wish to see in the world. 99

MAHATMA GANDHI

George and Josh arrived at the chamber of commerce the next morning to find the meeting room rapidly filling to capacity. It occurred to Josh that he had never asked about details of the lecture.

Josh inquired, "So what's the program? You mentioned it was something about leadership. Who's speaking?"

"I am," George said with a wink, "and the topic is Values-based Leadership."

Embarrassed, Josh didn't know what to say. He felt foolish for not seeking details sooner, and even more foolish for failing to connect the dots. "Well, break a leg," was all Josh could muster.

Locating a vacant seat near the front of the room, Josh exchanged pleasantries with the lady to his left and learned she was the executive director for a non-profit organization. To his right was the CEO of a local manufacturing firm.

Soon the chamber's president welcomed the audience and introduced George, concluding with, "No doubt you'll gain great benefit from his thoughts on *The Power of Values-based Leadership*. Please join me in welcoming Dr. George Greenfield!"

George walked briskly to the podium and turned to face the audience.

"I want to thank each of you for coming here today. I'm honored that you would give up such a beautiful Saturday morning to sit in on a lecture." George paused and clicked the projector remote control, illuminating the title slide:

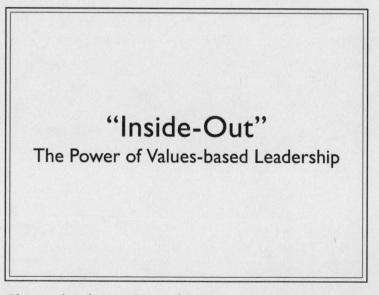

"Inside-Out"
The Power of Values-based Leadership

Clearing his throat, George began:

"I stand before you this morning ... the Imperfect Leader. Now, it's important to note that I didn't start out that way (he paused for chuckles from the audience)… like so many executives in all walks of life, my resume gives no hint of imperfection.

"In fact, my resume from almost thirty years in business suggests just the opposite. It proudly boasts of executive leadership excellence… positions of ever-increasing scope and responsibility, delivering exceptional results quarter after quarter… and then an interesting thing happened. About fifteen years ago a group of young managers asked me to teach them about leadership. We met every Friday for a year, studying the attributes of great leaders.

"Well, a wise man once said, 'To teach is to learn'…and learn I did… and the more I learned, the more I realized that *whatever* it was I had been practicing was *not* leadership. I came to understand my imperfections. I came to understand that if I wanted to make a difference…if I really wanted to impact society…if I truly wanted to leave a legacy…then something had to change…something inside of me. And so began my leadership journey.

"But the discussion today isn't about me…it *is* about transformational leadership concepts…and it *is* about you…men and women entrusted with the mantel of leadership." As a new slide appeared, George continued:

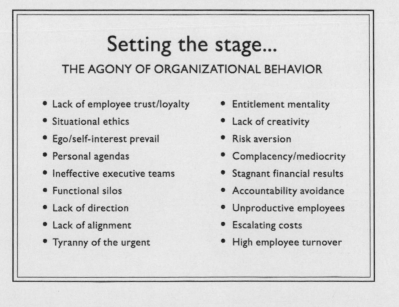

Setting the stage...
THE AGONY OF ORGANIZATIONAL BEHAVIOR

- Lack of employee trust/loyalty
- Situational ethics
- Ego/self-interest prevail
- Personal agendas
- Ineffective executive teams
- Functional silos
- Lack of direction
- Lack of alignment
- Tyranny of the urgent

- Entitlement mentality
- Lack of creativity
- Risk aversion
- Complacency/mediocrity
- Stagnant financial results
- Accountability avoidance
- Unproductive employees
- Escalating costs
- High employee turnover

"Before you is the 'Agony of Organizational Behavior.' These are undesirable and destructive behaviors that may be found in organizations and which negatively impact organizational performance.

"Perhaps the best way to teach something is to test and then teach. I wonder if you'd participate in a survey—testing, if you will—your frame of reference for our discussion. Take a moment to mentally place a check mark corresponding to those behaviors that are evident in your organization.

"Now, by a show of hands, how many of you checked three behaviors or more?" Almost everyone in the audience raised their hand.

"Six or more?" Still many hands remained in the air.

"Nine or more?" Almost a quarter of the audience had hands raised.

"We'll stop at nine to avoid potential embarrassment" (laughter rippled through the audience), "but I'd like you to take a moment to reflect how each of these behaviors affects the wellness of your company…how they affect your organization's ability to effectively execute your mission."

George paused, then resumed his comments: "Now I ask you to consider this: What if these conditions, or behaviors, did not exist? What if the situation was more positive?" Bringing up the following slide he continued:

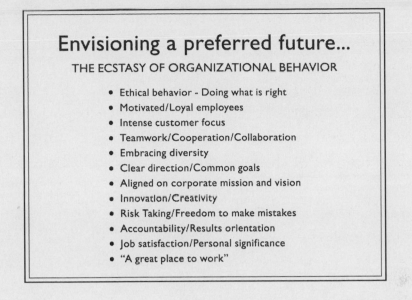

Envisioning a preferred future...

THE ECSTASY OF ORGANIZATIONAL BEHAVIOR

- Ethical behavior - Doing what is right
- Motivated/Loyal employees
- Intense customer focus
- Teamwork/Cooperation/Collaboration
- Embracing diversity
- Clear direction/Common goals
- Aligned on corporate mission and vision
- Innovation/Creativity
- Risk Taking/Freedom to make mistakes
- Accountability/Results orientation
- Job satisfaction/Personal significance
- "A great place to work"

"What if each of these 'Ecstasy' behaviors was prevalent in your organization? What would be the impact on customer satisfaction? On employee engagement and retention? On operational excellence? On long-term financial performance?

"I wonder…if these behaviors were the norm for U.S. corporations would we even recognize the names Sarbanes and Oxley?" (Nervous laughter from the audience.)

"What if I tell you," he continued, "that the 'Ecstasy of Organizational Behavior' *is* possible in every organization? Skeptics among you may be thinking that what I propose is a pipe dream…or at the very least that I took one too many valiums before addressing you this morning….(More laughter from the audience.)

"Today, I want to assure you these behaviors *are* possible!" Surveying the audience, George continued: "But it takes a certain kind of leader…" Here he paused for effect. "It takes a certain kind of leader to drive cultural change—the kind of change that influences organizational behavior. It takes a leader who envisions a preferred future for the organization and then leads from the inside-out to engage and motivate employees to execute well the organization's strategies and plans.

"So, what then, is an *inside-out* leader? And what is this Values-based Leadership rhetoric all about?

"*Inside-out* leaders lead with their core values. *Inside-out* leadership is about character; it's about who we are, what we believe and what we value.

"*Inside-out* leaders are values-based; that is, their personal behaviors result from personally held, core values. Values-based leaders understand that how they behave sets the example and establishes the model for organizational behavior. They understand that organizational behavior

It takes a certain kind of leader to drive cultural change—the kind of change that influences organizational behavior.

is the corporate culture. And they understand that *specific* behaviors generate predictable and sustainable results, enabling extraordinary organizational performance.

"Later we'll explore these values in detail, because possessing the *right* values is important. First let's examine the value proposition for Values-based Leadership."

George continued speaking, pointing as he talked to appropriate sections of the graphic displayed on the screen.

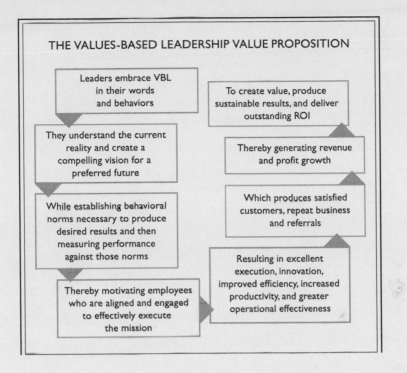

"What we're talking about here is a certain kind of leader, with a specific set of values, setting an explicit example. The values-based leader understands the current reality of the organization and creates a compelling vision for a preferred future while simultaneously establishing behavioral norms necessary to produce desired results, and then, measures performance against those norms.

"These employee behaviors become the organizational culture, motivating employees to increased levels of alignment and engagement. Employees then effectively execute the organization's mission—they exhibit creativity, drive, appropriate execution of strategies, and they deliver operational excellence.

"The result? Customers and clients are delighted with the company's products and services.

"The reward? Corporate financial goals are achieved and the company enjoys sustainable growth.

"The legacy? Value is created for employees, customers and shareholders, and the company produces exceptional return-on-investment.

"So now the question: Exactly what is Values-based Leadership? Values-based Leadership, or VBL as I like to call it, by definition is a leadership philosophy statistically proven to deliver exceptional results and extraordinary return-on-investment.

"I realize any big claim—especially one so contrary to conventional wisdom and divergent from current popular management practices—deserves support from a practical, well-documented business case.

"How many of you are familiar with Jim Collins' book *Good to Great?*"

A number of hands eagerly shot up from the audience.

"*Good to Great*, one of the best-selling business books of all time, is based on data compiled during a study of roughly 4,500 public companies. Collins and his team of MBAs discovered that about two dozen of those companies outperformed a robust stock market seven to one over a thirty-five-year period. Why?

"Conventional wisdom might suggest the stellar performances resulted from great strategies or from being in the right markets and industries, or perhaps from acquisitions. However, none of these scenarios was the case. Surprisingly, Collins discovered it was attributes of the leader that enabled and drove sustainable performance over extended periods of time. In fact, two attributes were common among the leaders of each *great* company. Collins said the attributes were 'absolute humility' and an 'iron will' to drive desired results.

"Another interesting study suggests values-driven organizations ultimately produce extraordinary results. In a landmark study on *Corporate Culture and Performance*, authors Kotter and Heskett documented how organizations that developed and managed a positive and strong culture—culture evidenced by living the values—significantly outperformed organizations that did not develop such a culture. Over a ten-year period revenue, stock price, net income, and job growth dramatically outperformed companies that lacked strong, positive cultures.

"Numerous other studies substantiate the benefits of Values-based Leadership. In fact, virtually any study on leadership trust, corporate culture, employee engagement, operational excellence, or

Values-driven organizations ultimately produce extraordinary results.

anything that measures a leader's impact on organizational performance can be linked to the VBL concepts.

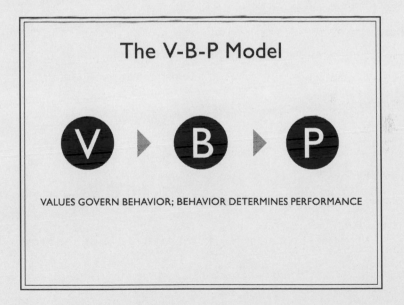

"Perhaps it's useful to consider a model to describe how VBL actually brings about exceptional performance. In the model on the screen 'V' stands for the agreed-upon values of an organization. 'B' is the organizational behavior indicative of those values. 'P' represents employee performance resulting from overall corporate behavior.

"I believe most of us have an intuitive sense for what values are the *right* values for a leader. After thirty years in business and many more years studying the topic, I've found values-based leaders possess and exemplify seven specific values. My list includes the values found on the next slide.

Values of the Values-based Leader

1. *Integrity:* They set an uncompromising example.

2. *Humility:* They selflessly serve and raise-up others.

3. *Compassion:* They care for others, demonstrate respect and develop potential in others.

4. *Purpose Driven:* They align with corporate mission, vision, and values; they inspire execution at every level.

5. *Courage:* They persevere to do the right thing.

6. *Self-Discipline:* They hold themselves and others accountable for operational performance.

7. *Gratitude:* They appreciate, acknowledge, and reward the contributions of others.

"Most people would readily agree on these values for values-based leaders. In fact, in even the most cursory review of mankind's top-ten religions—religions embraced by billions of people around the globe for centuries—it becomes readily apparent that there is a striking commonality in the values espoused. In short, the values of values-based leaders are intuitive. Whether the list I propose should be edited, or whether additions or deletions should be made, I'll leave for you to decide.

"At this point you may be asking yourself: Suppose I accept and embrace the values presented here…how do these values translate into organizational performance?"

Bringing the next slide to the screen George said, "A graphic aid expanding the V-B-P model may be useful….

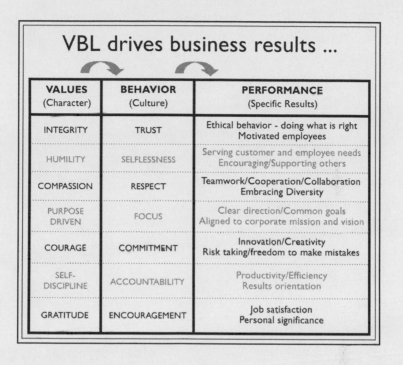

VALUES (Character)	BEHAVIOR (Culture)	PERFORMANCE (Specific Results)
INTEGRITY	TRUST	Ethical behavior - doing what is right Motivated employees
HUMILITY	SELFLESSNESS	Serving customer and employee needs Encouraging/Supporting others
COMPASSION	RESPECT	Teamwork/Cooperation/Collaboration Embracing Diversity
PURPOSE DRIVEN	FOCUS	Clear direction/Common goals Aligned to corporate mission and vision
COURAGE	COMMITMENT	Innovation/Creativity Risk taking/freedom to make mistakes
SELF-DISCIPLINE	ACCOUNTABILITY	Productivity/Efficiency Results orientation
GRATITUDE	ENCOURAGEMENT	Job satisfaction Personal significance

"VBL drives business results …"

"Beginning with the value of integrity we understand that the values-based leader will set an uncompromising example. When the leader consistently behaves with integrity, that behavior will be emulated, first by those closest to the leader, and then by others in the organization. When the leader behaves with integrity, he or she earns trust. As others emulate the leader, they too earn trust, first from the leader, and then from their peers and subordinates. As this practice permeates the organization a culture of trust evolves, and as integrity and trust become the norm, two things happen relative to organizational performance: First, employees throughout the organization practice ethical behavior and seek to do what is right—not what is expedient or convenient for short-term gain. Second, employees will experience new and heightened levels of motivation. Why? Because lack of trust is the number-one complaint of employees in organizations today. Create trust and you create motivated employees. Guaranteed.

"In similar fashion, let's consider the value of humility. When leaders consistently behave in a selfless fashion, focusing outside of themselves in an effort to serve and raise-up others with the goal of achieving organizational objectives, then those around them will emulate their example. As this behavior becomes widely imitated throughout the organization, a culture of selflessness takes hold. When selflessness becomes the norm among employees and leaders at all levels, the resulting performance is an intense customer focus and a devotion to meeting the needs of employees. Meanwhile, a culture evolves that dependably provides support and encouragement to all constituencies.

"In the instance of each value, the model works the same. The leader lives the value…followers emulate the value, thereby establishing a particular culture…and specific, predictable performance is the result.

"If this graphic looks vaguely familiar it is because the *Specific Results* listed here mirror exactly 'The Ecstasy of Organizational Behavior' we examined earlier." (Here George paused to allow time for reflection.)

"Living the values of a values-based leader may appear a daunting task. It's important to remember that no leader is perfect and that we're bound to make mistakes. One key to successfully becoming a values-based leader lies in your ability to enroll others to accompany you on the VBL journey. You will find fellow travelers to be a source of inspiration, encouragement, and accountability.

"A second key to becoming a values-based leader lies in understanding the secret of VBL. And the secret is this: There *is* one indispensable trait of a values-based leader and, as odd as it may seem, *humility* is the indispensable trait. Jim Collins proved this fact in his study.

"What is humility? First, what it is not: Humility isn't a foot-shuffling 'aw shucks' approach or false-modesty. It is not weakness. It is not believing that you are a 'nobody.'

"Webster's Dictionary defines humility as 'freedom from pride and arrogance; humbleness of mind; a modest estimate of one's own worth.'

"The bottom line on humility? It is the one indispensable trait of truly values-based leaders. Why? It's because leaders who demonstrate true humility are best able to motivate followers to high levels of execution and performance. And, as any good leader knows, it is performance that matters to organizational results."

> *Humility is the one indispensable trait of truly values-based leaders.*

George paused, surveying his audience.

"In conclusion, I would like to leave you with three thoughts.

"First, it takes a certain kind of leader with a specific set of values to create a strong corporate culture that executes well and achieves extraordinary results. Values-based leaders create and lead values-driven organizations that are energized, equipped, and organized to achieve powerful goals.

"Second: Humility precedes any success we may hope to achieve; it precedes any glory we might seek, and it precedes any honor that may come to us.

"Third: Each of us leads in one capacity or another. Some lead large corporations or divisions, functions, departments and teams within those corporations; some lead smaller companies; some lead charitable organizations, in a church or in the community; some lead military units or in government; certainly, as parents, you lead within your own homes.

> *Values-based leaders create and lead values-driven organizations that are energized, equipped, and organized to achieve powerful goals.*

"Departing today you may be certain that at one time or another, we each will lead…and we will do so imperfectly. But Values-based Leadership is worth the effort. I hope each of you will undertake the journey.

"You have been very kind. Thank you very much for your interest."

The audience broke into applause. As Josh clapped with the others, he somehow felt a part of George's lecture. He felt invigorated and rejuvenated.

Many in the audience stayed to ask questions; some desired a private word with George, others seemingly just wanted to remain in his presence. Almost forty-five minutes passed before the room cleared and the two men could depart.

As they drove home, Josh could hardly contain himself. "That was excellent," he exclaimed, "what a motivating lecture!"

"Thank you," George replied, "while the material is pertinent and true, I'm afraid my delivery is largely run-of-the-mill. However, I gratefully accept and sincerely appreciate your encouragement."

● ● ●

That evening Josh recounted George's lecture for Libby—as best he could. She seemed sincerely interested in the topic, although, truth be told, what fascinated her was her husband's apparent transformation. For months he had been reserved and subdued, almost depressed. Tonight he was animated and enthusiastic.

Late that night, Josh sat at his computer composing an e-mail to George.

From: jdmccall@emailxpress.com
Sent: Sunday, July 30, 2006 12:03 AM
To: greenfield@values.com
Subject: questions

George –

Where to begin? All afternoon and evening I've been thinking about your lecture. The message you delivered sounded so new and fresh, yet at the same time, somehow oddly familiar...it was easy for me to "connect." I've never before heard the case for values driving performance, but it makes intuitive sense to me. Like you implied in your lecture, the concept relates to something inside of me. While I'm eager to embrace the concepts because they seem so right, I do have several troubling questions....

Values seem like such a soft, "squishy" thing. Your model suggests that employees will voluntarily follow the example of their leader and that they then will readily adopt behaviors required by the organization to achieve strategic objectives... behaviors required to insure execution. It's not clear to me how this actually works. Am I missing something?

Another question is about the humility "thing." You gave definitions of humility, and you stressed its importance. I understand the concept, at least on the surface, but I need to understand what humility "looks like," manifested in actual behaviors, especially behaviors of leaders. How can a leader be humble and still be able to lead with strength, with confidence, and with authority?

In my e-mail the other day I asked how you see the

concepts of mission, values, and vision playing out on an organizational level. Your lecture helped me understand the impact of values in an organizational context, but I'm still unclear how individual mission, vision, and values fit into the organization's. Should they? Can they?

Finally, thank you for energizing me in such a significant way. Now what? Can we get together to talk?

Josh

The following afternoon Josh received George's reply:

From: greenfield@values.com
Sent: Sunday, July 30, 2006 4:59 PM
To: jdmccall@emailxpress.com
Subject: RE: questions

Dear Josh,

You're obviously a fast learner! Glad to hear that you are "energized," and yes, certainly we can talk further. Are you available tomorrow afternoon? The forecast is for rain (finally!), so it may be wise to find an indoor meeting place. If you enjoy coffee, perhaps we could go into town and talk at Bucks' Beanery. Would 2:30 p.m. be convenient?

Kindest regards,
G. Greenfield

SEVEN

> 66 Never separate doctrine from duty—
> we must never separate what we
> believe from how we behave. 99
>
> THOMPSON ALLEN

Driving into town to meet with George, Josh was grateful for the rain and hoped it would signal an end to the long summer drought.

Arriving promptly at 2:30, Josh found George seated in an overstuffed chair in the corner of the room, next to a massive stone fireplace. Josh waved to George before proceeding to the coffee bar. Returning with a large coffee-of-the-day, he settled into a chair adjacent to George. Without delay, he opened conversation: "So, what did you think of my questions?"

"Your questions were excellent," George replied with a broad smile.

"Well, thanks…what I mean is: What are your ideas about my questions?"

"Where would you like to begin?" George asked.

Deliberating for a moment, Josh began: "Why not start with the first one? Your case for values seemed convincing. It was truly motivating and I particularly liked the 'V-B-P' model. It makes sense…up to a point."

"Up to a point?" George asked.

The behavior of a leader is governed by who the leader is on the inside.

"Yes. It seems your position is that the behavior of a leader is governed by who the leader is on the inside; that is, he is governed by his values, and those who follow him will emulate his behavior, thereby resulting in a corporate culture—and that the aggregate behavior of followers, living out the culture, will result in specific desired performance. Am I correct so far?"

"Yes, go on," George said.

Josh continued, "Well, here's where I run into problems: It seems something is missing. It seems to me there is a huge leap from the leader's personal values to the notion of desired performance. Take, for example, the value of integrity. The leader behaves with absolute integrity, so now we expect the followers to automatically trust him and all fall in line to imitate his behavior, and then by some miracle we end up with motivated employees, ethical behavior, and people always doing what is right. It just can't be that easy…there's got to be something more. How do we know people will follow the leader's example? Where does behavior required of employees to achieve specific results fit in? Aren't required behavioral norms important?"

"You've certainly given the model much thought," George replied. "Behavioral norms are critically important for any organization to achieve desired results. Keep in mind that when I present the 'V-B-P' model I am addressing individual leaders, and behavioral norms are more or less implied in that approach, sandwiched between the 'B' and the 'P' of the model. Behavioral norms are the specific behaviors required of all employees—especially the leaders—to consistently comply with and live up to the stated values. These behavioral norms enable an organization to consistently deliver the specific performance necessary to achieve organizational goals—they are the behaviors by which corporate strategies are executed. Let's consider your example, the integrity value: What behavioral norms do you think would indicate integrity?"

Reflecting for a moment, Josh replied, "Doing what I say I'm going to do; telling the truth; doing what is right…that kind of thing."

"Yes, and what else?" prompted George.

"Telling the truth at all times; not compromising others; not filtering what is *real*; making sure my actions match my words."

"Indeed," George said, "and no doubt your list of behavioral norms could continue."

"Yeah, I guess it could," Josh agreed.

George continued: "I mentioned before that people 'want and need to be led'—they want to be led by someone they trust. Trust occurs when leaders daily model acceptable and agreed-upon behavioral norms…and you can be confident that whatever behavior is *lived out* by the leader will be imitated by the followers."

Josh interrupted, "I'm not so sure employees will copy the boss's behavior."

"That's a fair concern," George said. "Do you remember what you told me about Randy Ackerman, your boss at Trans Continental? Do you remember how you said he was an expert at corporate politics and the art of self-promotion, neither of which you felt was appropriate? Yet, what did you tell me about your behavior as a result of his example?"

Josh hesitated several long moments before answering and said, apparently speaking to the floor, "I told you that I started playing the political game and that I promoted myself and my abilities, even after leaving Trans Continental."

"And why did you do that, Josh?"

"Because," Josh replied, "...because I was impressed with Randy, and, initially, I trusted him. As a result, I suppose you might say I behaved like he behaved—in fact, I maintained elements of that behavior for years to come...I guess you made your point, George."

"And," George persisted, "if you have any doubts, simply consider more prominent examples of how followers emulate the example of their leader. On the positive side, consider Mahatma Gandhi and Martin Luther King, Jr., and the impact of their examples on followers. For another perspective, think about the leaders at Enron, Tyco, and the like. Do you not think followers at all levels in their organizations followed their examples? Routinely we find consistency between how a leader behaves and the behaviors and attitudes of their lieutenants."

"So let's say many employees *will* copy the behavior of their leader. Don't you think there always will be some people who won't follow the leader's example?"

"Certainly there always will be followers who do not emulate the leader's example," George answered. "That's why organizations create both formal and informal systems of rewards or punishments to reinforce expected behavior and insure compliance."

"Okay," Josh said in capitulation, "I get your point."

"Good, now let's set aside the topic of values to consider the elements of mission and vision," George said.

"Okay by me," Josh agreed, "but let me get a refill. Care for one?"

"That would be nice. A small decaf, please."

In Josh's absence, George drew two cloud-looking shapes on his napkin.

EIGHT

❝ The mark of an immature man is
that he wants to die nobly for a cause,
while the mark of a mature man is
that he wants to live humbly for one. ❞

WILHELM STEKEL

Josh returned with two steaming cups. He smiled when he noticed the drawing. "I knew we would get to the fun part eventually," he joked.

"Yes, eventually," George responded with a smile. "I just want to make sure I have your attention. But before we get to arts and crafts we need to discuss the importance of mission. Josh, why do you think corporations exist?"

Without hesitation, Josh offered: "To make a profit for shareholders."

"Yes," George replied, "certainly corporations need to provide return-on-investment for their owners and shareholders. But *why* does any company exist in the first place?"

"Oh, I see where you're going," Josh said. "Companies exist to provide livelihoods for their employees while delivering a product or service with the goal of providing a profit for the shareholders."

"Well, yes and no. I agree, Josh, corporations do in fact provide income for employees, and that profit may be the primary motivation for investors or shareholders; however, I don't necessarily agree that financial motivations are the reason for a company's existence."

"If not financial motivations, then *why do* companies exist?" Josh asked.

"Companies—or any organization for that matter—exist to fulfill human needs, or at least what we perceive to be our needs. For the sake of simplicity in reasoning, we might consider wants or desires and needs to be one and the same. To the extent a company accurately predicts human needs and provides products and services to meet those needs—

Companies—or any organization for that matter—exist to fulfill human needs.

and does so in a quality, cost-effective and efficient manner—then we as customers reward the company by purchasing its goods or services. It's only after the need is identified and met to the satisfaction of customers that financial rewards come into play. Therefore, a corporation, or again any organization, exists first and foremost to meet human needs."

Josh contemplated George's assumptions and then said, "Don't corporations specializing in personal investments exist just to make money?"

"On the surface it may seem that way, but ultimately the aim is providing for the client's financial *needs*," George countered. "Whether the need is for increased short-term cash flow, or to meet long-term needs such as a child's education, retirement, assisted-living expenses, etcetera, the ultimate goal is meeting a need."

"How about entertainment companies, like movie theaters, water parks, sports franchises…things like that?" Josh asked. "Don't they exist to make money? Certainly those are services that aren't actually *needed*, so the real reason they exist is to make money."

"Again, yes and no," George said. "It may be argued the companies of which you speak provide more for our wants rather than for actual needs, but the crux of the matter is that those companies ultimately meet very real human needs for relaxation, escape, enjoyment, and pleasure."

"So what you are saying is that any organization needs a reason to exist…it needs a purpose."

"Yes, Josh. Not long ago we talked about the fact that people require a personal *purpose* in which to find significance and fulfillment. We discussed how the notion of success isn't sufficient to provide fulfillment, but that success may be found when an individual pursues and realizes his or her purpose. In much the same way, money cannot be the reason corporations exist—they must identify and pursue a purpose that fulfills human needs.

"A company racing after money is like an individual running after success—neither can ever arrive at a final destination. Money, per se, cannot meet human needs—it merely provides a mechanism by which those needs are met. Success cannot fulfill an individual's need for fulfillment—it is

> *A company racing after money is like an individual running after success— neither can ever arrive at a final destination.*

simply a transitory measure of the quality of work and life experienced in her or his journey. So then, to achieve significance, organizations as well as individuals require a *purpose* to fulfill, and that purpose is described in terms of mission."

Josh sat deep in thought, sipping his coffee. After an extended silence he said, "What are the implications relative to leadership?"

"This," George began, "is where we discover how individual mission and corporate mission must fit together as the first step to effective leadership.

"Think back to the 80s, when 'corporate raiders' made headlines. From my limited understanding, these were wealthy, powerful individuals, or groups of individuals, who would prey on underperforming corporations with the intent of quickly returning the company to profitability and then 'flipping' it for huge profit. Usually the means to profitability were through divestitures of corporate assets, cut-backs, layoffs, and the like. Often the means employed had positive impact on the financial bottom line of the acquired company, yet rarely did the means do anything to improve customer satisfaction, nor did they enhance operational effectiveness or real efficiencies. Consider TWA as an example. It was acquired by a corporate raider who made severe cuts to drive financial performance. Subsequent management changes resulted in vain attempts to save the airline and eventually the company went out of business. Reviewing the carnage years later, we are hard pressed to suggest that TWA, its employees, or its customers are better off as a result of the corporate raider's initiatives.

"In the 90s, 'roll-ups' were the craze. In this scenario, investors purchased multiple, synergistic smaller companies, rolling them up into a larger organization. The idea was to create an organization that could capture larger market share and become a dominant, competitive force on a broad scale, while realizing 'back-office' and marketing efficiencies. Personally, I believe the investors' motives were to construct a larger and more profitable entity that could then be taken public or sold to a strategic buyer. Unfortunately, while many 'roll-ups' did bring extraordinary profits to investors, they didn't necessarily improve customer satisfaction, nor were they beneficial to the employees.

"In each case, the 'victim' companies were left with decreased ability to meet the needs of their primary constituencies: their customers and their employees. As a result, in each example the companies themselves frequently declined in value and effectiveness…and today either do not exist, or exist as mere shadows of their earlier prominence.

"So the question is why? I believe the answer lies in the motivation of the leaders. In the examples offered, I believe the acquiring leaders were financially motivated. They weren't driven by a corporation mission to meet specific needs, but by personal motivations to maximize wealth, and perhaps even power. As a result, long-term prospects for the companies were jeopardized because they no longer existed to achieve their initial stated missions: to meet specific human needs."

"Interesting," Josh said. "I never looked at it that way."

George continued: "Let's consider the other side of the coin. If we review the companies Jim Collins wrote about in *Good to Great*, we find that great organizations were guided by men and women who were aligned with and supportive of the company's stated mission. In fact, Collins suggests that these leaders possessed a resolve to insure the company's mission was achieved, above all else. Alignment of the leader's personal mission with that of the organization is critically important. When alignment exists, the potential also exists to create a great company. When there is lack of alignment…well, we already reviewed the consequences."

"This is hitting pretty close to home," interjected Josh. "Thinking back, I can clearly see how my own desire for achievement, influence, and recognition brought about involuntary separations and other professional hardships. Maybe I was more interested in my own mission than in that of the organization."

"Well, that's not for me to say," George gently replied. "But what

I do know is that introspection is important, and effective leaders must have keen self-awareness. Additionally, it's important to remember that one will be far more effective and productive as a leader if one sincerely aligns with the organization's mission, for the sake of the organization.

"As the saying goes, 'a rising tide floats all ships.' If the organization achieves its goals, almost by default, so too will the leader achieve his or her goals. But, the leader's personal mission must actually and sincerely be in sync with the corporate mission—it cannot be faked. Leaders will be able to achieve the desired goals only if they align with the corporate vision and values."

"So, what's the connection between the organization's vision and the leader?" Josh inquired.

"The answer to your question lies in having an accurate understanding of vision, and in the leader's awareness of his or her personal vision," George replied. "In fact, that's where my drawing on this napkin may be helpful. But first we should discuss the essence of vision. How would you define vision, Josh?"

"It seems to me," Josh began, "that vision has something to do with seeing the future. For organizations it probably means seeing what the organization looks like at some point in the future."

Vision is looking beyond the current reality and painting a picture of a preferred future, clearly bridging the gap between what is and what could or should be.

"Agreed. Vision is looking beyond the current reality and painting a picture of a preferred future, clearly bridging the gap between *what is* and *what could* or *should* be. Vision articulates the end game for an organization," George said.

"Why is vision so important, George?"

George responded with an old saying: "*If you always do what you always did, you'll always get what you always got.* In other words, lack of vision commits an organization to remain firmly entrenched in its current reality…and for most organizations, maintaining the status quo is unacceptable for achieving the necessary growth to accomplish their stated missions.

"Vision begins with the leader's unwillingness to accept things the way they are. This restiveness is essential because vision motivates followers with promise of a preferred future; it serves as a guiding compass; it creates alignment of effort; it unleashes creativity and innovation; it insures focus on what really matters, and compels the organization to discern *best* from *good*. Vision gives meaning to work."

"I see its importance," Josh said. "So how do you see the leader's role vis-à-vis the organization's vision?"

"The leader plays several critical roles," George replied. "The senior leader is the *originator* of the vision, although he or she must never create it in a vacuum. Compelling visions usually arise from the collective passions of leaders and followers at all levels in the organization—passions that cause people to dream about and strive for what could be. This yearning fuels the fire for a preferred future and provides avenues for professional and personal significance. Wise leaders connect with and capture these collective passions, incorporating them into a corporate vision that can be widely embraced.

"The leader is also *cheerleader* for the vision. She or he repeatedly paints the picture for a preferred future and

> *The pursuit of a preferred future is seldom easy and is often risky. Safe and easy are bywords of the status quo—they are attitudes that almost guarantee things will remain the same.*

demonstrates the courage required to step into the unknown, taking necessary risks as catalysts for action. The pursuit of a preferred future is seldom easy and is often risky. *Safe* and *easy* are bywords of the status quo—they are attitudes that almost guarantee things will remain the same.

"Finally, the senior leader is the primary *communicator* of the vision. It's imperative that the senior leader clearly articulate the vision in a manner readily embraced and easily remembered by the organization's rank-and-file—and this task is rarely accomplished by way of a vision statement. Words alone are insufficient to motivate performance. Leaders must learn to articulate vision through pictures, symbols, and stories, the means that best connect with people's passions."

Josh jumped in, "And I suppose your last comment brings us to your work of art on this napkin?"

"Indeed it does," George said with a chuckle. Taking a moment to sketch several icons, he continued:

"Let's imagine a regional medical-supply company with this mission: *Premiere healthcare products for all.* The leader's job is to create a vision that will mobilize and inspire employees to achieve a compelling, preferred future for the organization. In this vision we see picture elements suggesting healthcare as a focus, global impact, and work that brings personal and professional significance to every individual in the company. A good vision picture probably will include other symbols, and more detail, but, no doubt, you get my point."

"I do," Josh said. "What is the significance of the smaller *cloud-thing?*"

"That represents the leader's personal vision. It is vitally important that the leader's personal vision is in complete harmony with the vision he or she originates for the organization. If alignment is lacking, it's impossible for the leader to exemplify behaviors that will enable successful realization of the corporate vision. The two will be at odds and the leader will fail…or, worst case, be considered a fraud."

Excitedly, Josh interjected, "What you're describing is a superb example of my situation at National Service Masters. If the CEO had been honest with himself about his vision for a preferred future, his *vision-cloud* for the company would have been full of dollar signs, all pointing to icons representing the executive team. My version of the vision would have symbols representing market growth, energized employees, and satisfied customers. Obviously there was a disconnect… and in this case, I was the one that failed, because I couldn't, or wouldn't, align with the CEO's vision!"

"Yes Josh, this is a first-hand example of how corporate vision must connect with a leader's vision. However, you shouldn't be too hard on yourself. From what you described at National Service Masters, I sincerely doubt any of the company's employees—except the benefiting executive team—would embrace the CEO's vision."

"And as a result," Josh added, "it's little wonder that National Service Masters is in the same market position, with the same revenues, as when I left the company over four years ago."

"Exactly," George agreed. "Visionary leaders stimulate and bind together the dreams of employees in an organization, creating unity by means of a compelling vision that connects each of their personal visions to one another, and to the organization.

Visionary leaders stimulate and bind together the dreams of employees in an organization, creating unity by means of a compelling vision.

Creativity, innovation, employee engagement, and outstanding execution are the results."

"I think I'm beginning to understand," Josh remarked. The next step is values… right?"

"Correct. But, given the time, that's a conversation for another day," George said.

The two men conversed awhile longer and departed, agreeing to meet the following week.

Josh returned home a bit overwhelmed. The things George said were profound and somewhat disturbing. They seemed so *right*, so intuitive, so simple, and so potentially effective—but embracing the concepts would necessitate a paradigm shift for Josh. Many of George's thoughts were inconsistent with what Josh observed in the *real* world—but he had to admit the validity of George's reasoning.

NINE

> **"** If we keep treating our most
> important values as meaningless relics,
> that's exactly what they'll become. **"**
>
> MICHAEL JOSEPHSON

The following week George and Josh resumed their conversation at Bucks' Beanery. Revisiting the topic of values, Josh said, "I'm still a little fuzzy on the connection between the leader's personal values and how they influence organizational performance."

"Perhaps you'll allow me a bit of a lecture as I attempt to clarify," George suggested. "We start with the premise that values-based leaders create and lead values-driven organizations that are energized, equipped, and organized to achieve exceptional performance. A values-based organizational culture can only be established when people embrace the need for change in the way they interact with each other. And these changed interactions must necessarily follow the demonstrated change and commitment of those who guide, direct, and serve the organization. The change must begin with the leader, or leaders. If leadership fails to embody the values, then no one will follow.

> *If leaders fail to embody the values, then no one will follow.*

"Many business leaders believe the right marketing, technological, and operational strategies coupled with specific revenue, profit, expense, and market-share goals, will drive corporate performance. Granted, strategy and goals are important, but they will be ineffective in delivering desired performance if not executed by aligned and motivated employees.

"The single-most important determinant of corporate results is corporate culture. Culture is determined by a *willingness* on the part of employees to align their attitudes and beliefs with the intent and desires of executive management. Therefore, to positively impact corporate performance, leaders must live out personal values. By their example they then inspire *willingness* on the part of employees to emulate desired behaviors. Without such voluntary alignment, no brilliant strategy or worthy goal can be achieved.

"How employees *feel* about their jobs, the significance of their work and their relationship with their boss and coworkers—and what they *believe* about standards of acceptable behavior and accountability for results—have a critical impact on the organization's ability to deliver expected results. Why?"

"Because," Josh interjected, "how employees *feel* and what they *believe* are predicated upon values. And, as I'm beginning to understand, employee behaviors resulting from those values determine organizational performance."

"Precisely," George agreed. "Too many leaders fail to understand the key to desired results lies in their ability to grasp the critical relationship between corporate culture and potential for future success. In fact, corporate culture is the primary determinant of what can be achieved. Therefore, leaders must understand the realities

> *Corporate culture is the primary determinant of what can be achieved.*

of their current cultural environment and proactively influence that culture to greater effectiveness. The influencing process begins with values; however, to make the values come alive in hearts and minds, *behavioral norms* must be established for employees to adequately understand *how* to live the values."

"The influencing process...so that's where behavioral norms come into play," Josh mused.

"Indeed," George said as he extracted a pen from his pocket and began to draw on a napkin. "The influencing process works something like this.

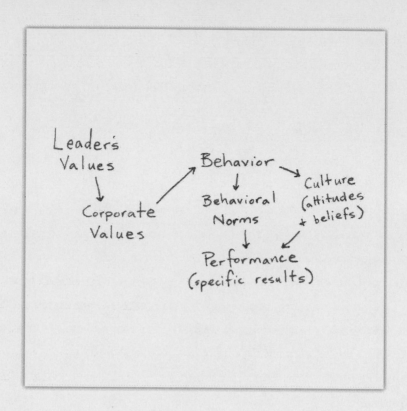

"The leader *naturally* brings her or his personal values to the organization. When establishing a value-set for the organization, the leader first must identify personal values embraced by employees-at-large and by the executive team. Through a collaborative process, commonly held values are vetted and ultimately become the corporate values. Once corporate values are established, the executive team commits to alignment on, and accountability for, living out those values, thereby influencing—by their behavior—the employees' beliefs about what behaviors are required.

"Because corporate values may appear indistinct or imprecise, it's necessary to establish behavioral norms to elucidate specific behaviors expected relative to each value. When behavioral norms are spelled out in this manner, they become the corporate standard for acceptable performance, which in turn enables predictable execution and sustainable results."

Josh broke in: "It does seem logical that values described in terms of specific behaviors become something employees can embrace and act on."

"Absolutely," George concurred. "Values allow for great diversity within an organization because they provide context

Values described in terms of specific behaviors become something employees can embrace and act on.

for a deep, underlying unity. Unity and diversity are imperative for innovation, creativity, and risk-taking, and these elements combined are essential to achieve aggressive, significant goals. Therefore, the commonality of accepted values and subsequent behavioral norms are the secret to transformational change."

"Okay, okay…I'm coming around to your point of view," Josh said, smiling. "But I have one more question."

"And that would be?" George asked.

Josh continued, "It's this: Let's assume that the leader's personal values are similar to what you call the *right* values—and I assume you mean VBL values. Thinking of corporate values of companies I worked for, it seems to me none were identical to those you espouse for VBL."

"Quite right," George said with an encouraging nod. "In fact, seldom if ever will you find corporate values identical to VBL values. Organizations almost never create values identical to those I proposed. However, a strong correlation does exist."

Flipping over the napkin, George asked, "Can you remember a specific set of corporate values at one of your previous employers?"

"Sure," Josh replied. "At ChemExperts we were required to memorize them. They were *Integrity, Performance, Teamwork,*

Innovation, and *Respect for People*."

As Josh spoke, George wrote on the napkin.

<u>Corporate Values</u> <u>VBL Values</u>

- Integrity ⟶ Integrity

- Performance ⟶ Purpose driven + self Discipline

- Teamwork ⟶ Humility

- Innovation ⟶ Courage

- Respect for People ⟶ Compassion + Gratitude

"If you consider VBL values in a broad context," George began, "I think it's apparent there's a direct connection between ChemExperts' values and VBL values. In fact, over the years I conducted an informal study and found this similarity usually exists. Furthermore, I believe the values espoused in VBL are virtually intuitive and are widely embraced by people throughout the world."

"But what if they're not?" Josh argued. "What if similar values are not embraced by an individual, or group of individuals?"

"Certainly," George countered, "there are individuals and groups of individuals that defy condoned behavior. They run to the beat of a different and contrary drummer. While those people certainly exist, I emphatically believe they're neither the norm, nor the majority. One job of the values-based leader is to either influence nonconformists to change for the sake of the whole, or to remove them from the organization. Isn't that what we do with people who live contrary to society's laws? Don't we remove them for the sake and well-being of the whole?"

"You're probably right," Josh said. "So, *if* the *right* values are pretty much intuitive, they'll be accepted readily by most responsible individuals and probably will be evident in the values statements of organizations."

"That summary would indeed be accurate as to my position," George concurred with a smile. "Enough for one day?"

"Enough for one day," Josh agreed.

• ● •

That evening Josh and Libby talked late into the night. He told her about the conversation with George, complete with an attempt to replicate George's drawings.

"Josh, honey," Libby asked, "What does all this mean to you? You seem so excited…so energized. What are you going to do with it all…with all that you're thinking?"

"That's a good question," Josh replied, "What do *you* think I should do?"

"If you're asking me what kind of job you should pursue, or what industry you should work in," Libby answered, "I don't know what to say. I *do* know that whatever you do, you always manage to end up in a leadership position. People trust you. They know you care, and they value the way you try to make a difference. Josh, you can't ignore the fact that you're driven to lead."

After sitting in silence, Libby finally interrupted Josh's thoughts: "Josh, what do you think *you* should do?"

"Frankly, I'm not sure…. Actually, I don't have a clue what I'll end up doing."

Suddenly changing her tone, Libby blurted, "You don't have a clue?" Obviously frustrated, she continued: "Josh, I thought you were meeting with George to figure it out…to find a job! You've *got* to figure it out. That you're trying to *find* yourself is all well and good…but, Josh, we need answers…."

"I know," Josh replied. "And I desperately want to find the answer, but at this point I just don't know what the answer is. I am clear about this: If I can identify my purpose, then everything else should fall into place—the job, my ability to support you and the kids, and maybe even the opportunity to make a difference."

More relaxed, Libby asked: "What did George say about your purpose?"

"Actually," Josh replied, "he didn't address my specific purpose. He spoke in more general terms. He explained that we find purpose once we articulate and pursue our mission, vision, and values, and that these elements guide us to answer the question of what we're trying to do. George *did* ask me what I'm trying to do—and then he asked me what it is about *me* that is standing in the way."

"Why would he ask such rude questions?"

"Libby, I'm beginning to realize the questions weren't rude at all. In fact, George's questions demand an answer—if I'm going to figure out what to do with my life."

"If that's the case," Libby asked, "what does that mean about a job?"

We find purpose once we articulate and pursue our mission, vision, and values, and these elements guide us to answer the question of what we're trying to do.

"I'm not sure, exactly. Maybe the first steps are to learn more about the Values-based Leadership philosophy and understand how it applies to me."

Surmising the answer, Libby smiled and posed a final question: "And how do you do *that*, Joshua David McCall?"

"Well…I start by asking George, of course."

TEN

“ Be careful of your thoughts,
For your thoughts become your words;
Be careful of your words,
For your words become your deeds,
Be careful of your deeds,
For your deeds become your habits;
Be careful of your habits,
For your habits become your character;
Be careful of your character,
For your character becomes your destiny. ”

FRANK OUTLAW

From: jdmccall@emailxpress.com
Sent: Monday, August 7, 2006 9:17 PM
To: greenfield@values.com
Subject: "How do I ..."

George –

These past few weeks have been quite an awakening for me. After our last conversation Libby and I spent hours going over the things you and I talked about. What became apparent was this: I need to better define my purpose...which probably means I must understand my passion in life and the values I embrace. I believe that it (my passion) has something to do with leadership, but I still need to gather thoughts and sort thru specifics. Also, I very much want to better understand VBL, and how to do it well. It's important to me to help create a values-based organization, wherever I end up.

Josh

George's reply:

From: greenfield@values.com
Sent: Monday, August 7, 2006 10:01 PM
To: jdmccall@emailxpress.com
Subject: RE: "How do I ..."

Dear Josh,

I'd be delighted to share my thoughts. In your e-mail you referred to "passion in life" and "values"—each comes from within. What's embedded on the "inside" is ultimately what comes to the surface. If one is dissatisfied and unfulfilled with one's life and circumstances, resolution begins with transformation of that which is "within."

Josh, your questions are important—they are critical to your journey. The things you are passionate about are key elements to understanding your purpose. So, too, is understanding your character—the manifestation of your values—and the first step of the process lies in self-awareness. Why not take a stroll tomorrow to discuss? Would you care to join me at 3 PM, by the lake?

Kindest regards,
G. Greenfield

• ● •

The next day George and Josh met by the now familiar oak, on the bank of the small lake. After greetings and brief chitchat, eager to pursue George's thoughts, Josh began: "In your e-mail you introduced the topic of character. Is that a new twist on the VBL philosophy?"

"Not really," George answered, "it primarily is implied in our earlier conversations. How we interpret our current circumstances and how we see the past, or the future for that matter, is the result of what we have become in our character. Character is formed from a compilation of all our previous life experiences, environmental stimuli, and personal interactions—the influences that shape our values. Character is what defines *who* we are at the very core of our being.

> *Character is what defines who we are at the very core of our being.*

"Character is vitally important, especially for leaders. Character determines whether a leader will succeed or fail. Warren Bennis once wrote, 'Research at Harvard University indicates 85 percent of a leader's performance depends on personal character.' Ultimately, the leader's character is *the* determinant of a follower's willingness to follow. It is a matter of trust—more compelling than either vision or mission. A leader's character is the result of his or her personal values."

"If the statistics Bennis quoted are accurate," Josh observed, "then it's literally tragic that traditional leadership development focuses almost exclusively on outward, observable skills, with little or no attention to the question of character."

"What's on the inside matters more than anything else to answer what we are to become. The first challenge is to know what's on the inside," George said.

"You're talking about self-awareness, aren't you?" Josh asked.

"Yes. Self-awareness accords you the benefit of understanding what you care about, what drives you, what your abilities, giftedness, and aptitudes are. Self-awareness acts as an internal compass and gives direction. Self-awareness also allows you to look back and objectively take responsibility for past failures, while enabling you to learn from mistakes. And, keen self-awareness implies individual mastery of one's personal mission, vision, and values."

Josh groaned. "Sometimes I feel like we're going around in circles," he said.

"True," George responded, "it might appear that way, and in a sense we are. Your values establish *who you are* and *what you care about*, thereby providing the core from which springs your life's mission, or that which affords you personal significance. Personal significance is achieved when you transcend your current reality to a preferred future—your vision. Self-awareness is the catalyst that enables you to clearly understand, embrace, and act upon your values, mission, and vision. In the absence of accurate self-awareness, the wrong values may surface, personal missions can be imprecise, and vision unclear…and most likely will lead down a path of frustration, restlessness, discontent, disillusionment, and a general lack of fulfillment.

"And it is in this unhappy situation that we find too many people, especially leaders: They are not *in touch* with themselves—they are not *true* to themselves. As a consequence, they sell out to the wrong values, behaving contrary to what is virtuous and good;

> *In the absence of accurate self-awareness, the wrong values may surface, personal missions can be imprecise, and vision unclear.*

instead pursuing power, position, personal wealth, prestige, ambition, etcetera—all of which lead to a lust for more, and to a longing that can never be satisfied.

"Self-awareness, coupled with self-discipline, enables focus on that which is good: Earning authority instead of seeking power; desiring influence over position; creating value rather than accumulating wealth; preferring honor over prestige; and seeking to serve rather than using others to serve personal ambitions.

"Ironically, by living out the *right* values, the personal greatness one seeks can be achieved and most certainly will exceed what would come about by living the *wrong* values. It is a fact documented in the life of every truly great leader who had a positive impact on the history of mankind."

"That seems like a pretty big claim," interjected Josh. "I mean your statement about the right values being lived out by every great leader in history."

"Yes," George said, "it is a big claim. Let's look at some examples to explore my supposition. Can we first agree that in general, VBL values are the *right* values and that for the sake of our discussion, values contrary in principle to VBL would be the *wrong* values?"

"That makes sense to me," Josh agreed.

"Can we also agree to three qualifiers?" George asked. "First, to be considered a truly great leader the individual must have impacted society in transformational ways; second, the accomplishments of these leaders are internationally recognized; and third, can we accept that while they strive to live the *right* values, almost all leaders—even the greatest ones—are no doubt imperfect in one way or another?"

"Again agreed," Josh said.

George thought for a moment and then went on: "Thinking about truly great leaders, it's interesting to note the most prominent examples are national figures of some sort. While I'm confident numerous examples of values-based leaders exist in the business world, none come readily to mind who meet our first two qualifiers."

"Then who are some of the leaders who *do* qualify?" Josh asked.

"Well, beginning in our own country, a notable example is George Washington who, despite tremendous odds, deserves much credit for establishing the United States as a nation, and for enabling civil and religious liberty.

"Next," George said, "we might consider Nelson Mandela in South Africa, who made a legendary stand at great personal sacrifice to lead efforts that resulted in breaking the grip of apartheid. In England, William Wilberforce took an unpopular political stand to abolish England's slave trade and to restore a sense of morals to his country."

Josh concurred with the selections as George continued: "In each case, these leaders were intently focused on and *purpose driven* toward their missions; each demonstrated extreme *courage, integrity* and, no doubt, incredible *self-discipline*. Also, by their voluntary submission to suffering or by enduring uncomfortable circumstances, each exhibited *humility*.

"Two names in India come to mind for inclusion as truly great leaders: The first is Mother Teresa, who is known worldwide for gaining international support to care for widows, orphans, the homeless, and the sick. She perhaps is the epitome of what *compassion* and *humility* look like in a leader. Also from India was Mahatma Gandhi, who, breaking the yoke of British domination, peacefully led a fifth of humanity to independence and helped to found the largest democracy in the history of the world. He, too, offers a supreme example of *courage*, *humility*, and being *purpose driven*."

"It is interesting that two on your list were in India," Josh remarked.

"Yes," George replied, "and it is even more interesting—perhaps ironic—that each would tell you their role model was Jesus. It is interesting because each chose to emulate Jesus' behavior. It is ironic because, while Mother Teresa and Gandhi were not aligned on faith issues, they certainly were aligned on the quality of Jesus as a leader."

"An interesting observation," Josh added.

"No matter what one believes about *who* Jesus is, his influence and impact are undeniable and his legacy unsurpassed by any other leader. Looking back twenty centuries, if we evaluate his influence, we realize no other leader has come close to Jesus' effect on human history and his impact on mankind.

"The question is how? While obviously there is more to the answer, from a leadership perspective, it is because he led perfectly. Jesus was passionate about—and committed his life to—a worthy mission; he offered a compelling vision for a preferred future; and he truly *lived out*, on a daily basis, all the values we attribute to Values-based Leadership."

"That's a lot to take in and think about" Josh said.

And then, as if on cue, his cell phone rang. Answering the call, Josh discovered Matthew missed the bus home from school and needed a ride. Apologizing to George, Josh excused himself as George agreed to continue the conversation the following afternoon.

ELEVEN

66 The paradox of self-awareness is that
one cannot become self-aware by self alone. 99

DEPAK SEPTHI

Reconvening near the lake, George lost no time refocusing their discussion on self-awareness. He reminded Josh of his comments from the day before, highlighting his belief that self-awareness is the catalyst that enables people to clearly understand, embrace, and act upon their values, mission, and vision, enabling focus on that which is good.

"At the risk of being rude," Josh said, "that leads back to my original question of how to reevaluate—how to become self-aware."

"Ah, I apologize, Josh. I tend to lecture at times, don't I?"

Grinning, Josh replied: "Maybe a little, but your lectures do give me food for thought...."

"Self-awareness is both art and science—art in that one never truly knows if or when one arrives at a perfect state; science in that there are proven processes and instruments that can greatly aid the endeavor."

"Like what?" Josh asked.

"Well, in the case of values, you might write down all the principles, ideals, and standards you think you embrace, without casting judgment as to legitimacy or correctness. Next, create a list of behaviors indicative of each. Once completed, the list of behavioral norms you selected as compatible with what you truly believe will guide you to an associated value, thereby revealing your personal value-set."

"George, I'm a visual learner; do you have any napkins to draw on? I think I could benefit from an example."

Chuckling, George pulled a notepad from his coat pocket and began to write. "Let's appraise two values," he suggested. "We'll start with integrity. Associated with integrity are behavioral norms such as doing what you say you are going to do; doing what is right; telling the truth at all times; making sure your actions match your words. Would you say you are willing to commit yourself to living according to those behaviors?"

"Well, sure," Josh said, "who wouldn't?"

> ## Integrity
> Doing what I say I'm going to do;
> doing what is right;
> telling the truth at all times;
> making sure actions match words.
>
> ## Wealth
> Diligently pursuing substantial income;
> striving to achieve financial status;
> amassing large capital reserves;
> living in a luxurious home;
> accumulating material possessions.

"Fine," George continued, "integrity tends to be a universally accepted value. Next, we'll consider the value of wealth, with the associated behaviors of pursuing substantial income; striving to achieve financial status; amassing large capital reserves; living in a luxurious home; and accumulating material possessions. Would you say you are willing to commit yourself to living according to those behaviors?"

Josh studied the list and responded: "Wealth certainly isn't a bad thing and might be nice to achieve and enjoy, but I'm not sure I'd be willing to commit my life to those behaviors. If I lived merely to exemplify the wealth behaviors, the cost might be too great in terms of family, friendships, health, well-being, reputation, etcetera."

"That's precisely my point," George said. "Based on your responses, you would then select integrity as one of your personal values, while deselecting wealth. The fact that an ideal or principle is not included in your value-set is not a judgment as to its worthiness or desirability; it simply means that it does not rate as a driving force in *who* you are—at the core."

"So once this exercise is completed it seems what's left—after the select-deselect process—is my personal value-set."

Self-awareness of mission evolves when one first establishes the foundation of personal values and lays upon it an understanding of his passions, interests, aptitudes, and personality.

"If the exercise is honestly completed, that should be the case," George affirmed. "Having reflected on ways to determine personal values, we can now focus on mission. Self-awareness of mission evolves when one first establishes the foundation of personal values and lays upon it an understanding of his passions, interests, aptitudes, and personality."

"Right," Josh interjected, "I've taken numerous personality and competency assessments throughout the years—things like Myers-Briggs, DiSC, Strong's Interest Survey and the CAPS abilities assessment."

"And all are excellent, thoroughly validated, and useful instruments, but I have found them lacking; they don't create a portrait of the *whole person*. That's why I use a new assessment that looks at an individual in the areas of mission, competency, and personality, and then converges those dimensions into a holistic portrait of the individual—it's called PRO Development."

"Really, tell me more," prompted Josh.

George continued: "The assessment provides a fascinating picture of an individual's strengths and ideal roles, coupling that information with the individual's preferred corporate culture. Another interesting facet of the instrument is an almost uncanny ability to suggest a *core theme*, or personal mission statement for the individual. At any rate, my point is that it is important to take advantage of such instruments because they give vital clues to your overall mission."

"Moving ahead…how does all this relate to vision?" Josh asked.

"Vision is a bit more elusive," George replied. "It comes about over time, as one pursues mission. It stems from dissatisfaction with current reality and becomes the catalyst for a preferred future. In a personal context, it's a picture much like the one I drew on the back of a napkin at Bucks' Beanery—I believe you referred to it as a *cloud-thing*. Within the *cloud-thing*, you should create icons that reflect what you want your end-game—your legacy—to look like."

"George, can you give me an example of what would be in the picture?"

"Perhaps the easiest example," George said, "would be from my own vision. My *cloud-thing* includes icons representing a strong marriage and family, an extensive network of family, friends, associates, and professional contacts, international travel, reliance on my faith, focus on the issue of leadership, and, finally, an icon representing personal influence that positively impacts society. It's my attempt to graphically portray what I want my life to look like—my end game."

"Your vision certainly is more compelling than *he who dies with the most toys wins*," Josh joked.

"That's my fervent hope. I believe life is about relationships—nothing more, nothing less… relationships between spouses, between family members, between friends, between leaders and followers, between employees and customers, between members of society, between Creator and created.

> *Life is about relationships—nothing more, nothing less…. How we address and impact those relationships determines our legacy.*

How we address and impact those relationships determines our legacy. In the final analysis, the only thing of lasting value is the influence and positive impact we have on others, and that impact is determined by the quality of our relationships."

"That's deep," Josh said, half serious, half chiding, "and actually,

I've heard it before. People often say it's relationships that matter, but you sure wouldn't know it by the way most people act."

"Unfortunately, that's true," George said. "Too often we tend to *interact* with people rather than to *relate* with them. *Interacting* implies acting upon others, while *relating* suggests connecting with or responding favorably to them. No doubt the difference is subtle, yet important. When we *interact*, the goal inevitably is to get what we want. When we *relate* our focus is on the other person, either for mutual advantage or solely for their benefit. In which case do you think people respond most favorably to us?"

"Obviously, when we relate with people," Josh answered.

"And in which case do you believe people will most likely connect with our values, beliefs, ideas, goals, or aspirations?" George asked.

"Again, when we have a relationship with them," Josh said.

"So then," George continued, "doesn't it make sense that quality relationships are imperative to our ability to leave a legacy?"

"I don't know," Josh said. "Isn't life about achieving goals, about creating value, about accomplishing something?"

"To some extent that may be accurate," George replied, "but the question is: For what purpose do you do those things? For whom do you achieve goals, create value, and accomplish things?"

Josh thought for a moment and answered: "Ultimately, I suppose, if I answer altruistically, it's so our families will be better off, or in some way, to make the world a better place...."

George interrupted: "And the self-aware leader understands the critical importance of building strong relationships to achieve those goals. We need other people to help us accomplish our vision for a preferred future, and we must establish relationships with others if we hope to enlist their support to carry out the task. Self-awareness helps us realize that we must adapt the way we relate to others in order to make a personal connection that encourages others to participate in our journey."

"Okay, let me talk through this: The process of self-awareness will create the framework for my personal values, mission, and vision. It can improve the quality of my relationships, which in turn positively impacts my influence over others and eventually results in a life of significance as evidenced by the legacy I leave," Josh summarized.

"Yes and no," suggested George. "Self-awareness is not the entire issue. It is but one leg of a three-legged stool. In my e-mail, I alluded to a process. *Awareness* is the first step in the process. The second is *Alignment*, and *Accountability* is the third."

Continuing, George said, "Articulating personal values, mission, and vision vis-à-vis personal self-awareness is the first step in the process. The second is a commitment to aligning those elements with the way you live your life. In other words, you bring your behavior into alignment with your stated values; you seek vocation consistent with your mission; you undertake only those pursuits that will move you toward successful realization of your vision. The challenges here are of focus and discipline, and the inevitable question is: Will you make choices consistent with your values, mission, and vision?"

"Judging from my past," Josh interjected, "it seems that I may not always make the right choices."

George continued: "Too often individuals—and, tragically, leaders—subjugate their inner beliefs and desires to pursue the gods of elusive success, insatiable monetary gain, and an unquenchable thirst for power or prestige. The result? Lack of fulfillment, unrealized potential, and the lack of personal significance, for themselves and for their

> *Will you make choices consistent with your values, mission, and vision?*

followers. Josh, finding success in the journey and leaving a personal legacy, requires one to be true to self...."

"And the third step in the process?" Josh was eager to learn more.

"The third step," George said, "is perhaps the most challenging of all. *Accountability* is required if we are to put into practice that to which we say are aligned. Accountability suggests either an obligation or willingness to be held responsible, accountable, or liable for our actions and deeds. It is the position in which we place ourselves to be answerable to someone or something—and accountability must come from the *outside*."

"From outside the individual, or outside the organization?" Josh asked.

"Both," George replied. "By definition accountability comes from outside the individual. We're *accountable* when we grant someone permission to tell us *We simply don't see ourselves the way others see us, and we cannot exactly discern the impact of our words and actions on others.* what they see and hear in our actions and words. Actually, it's a matter of practicality: Human beings by nature are insufficiently self-aware and lack the self-discipline to accomplish the task of accountability on our own. We simply don't see ourselves the way others see us, and we cannot exactly discern the impact of our words and actions on others. It's not an issue of intent, but of capability.

"Despite good intentions, we sometimes buckle under stress or external influence, and may be tempted to compromise our values or mission, and subsequently become misaligned with *what it is we are trying to do*. In these instances it isn't unusual for us to rationalize, or attempt to justify our words and actions. Consequently, we need an unbiased observer to provide input and feedback—someone to help us stay on course toward the values we espouse, the objectives we pursue, and the commitments we have made. Ideally, it should be someone we trust and respect, and someone who has our best interests in mind."

"Should that unbiased observer be internal or external to the organization?" Josh asked.

"Not to be flippant," George replied, "but again my answer—especially in the case of senior executives—is…*both*. Leaders need clear, constructive, and honest feedback if they desire to maximize their leadership effectiveness. Sometimes the best feedback is provided by those within the organization because they have first-hand knowledge of the impact of the leader's words and actions. It is essential for the leader to create an accountability culture and open environment from which such input is readily forthcoming—from the executive team and from employees."

Josh considered George's comments and asked, "If a leader can be held accountable by constituencies within the organization, why would he want someone external to the organization to hold him accountable?"

"Several reasons," George said. "Sometimes, despite sincere efforts, the leader simply doesn't receive accurate or timely feedback. Often, an external observer can provide superior insights *because* they are external to the environment and have a different perspective, unfettered by internal biases or preconceived notions. Often, leaders seek outside accountability partners because they want someone in whom they can confide…someone with no personal agendas, ulterior motives or organizational ambitions…someone who listens without judging, offers encouragement…or serves as a sounding board.

"Whatever the case, it's lonely at the top and astute executives understand they cannot go it alone—effective leaders want and seek

> *It's lonely at the top and astute executives understand they cannot go it alone— effective leaders want and seek wise counsel.*

wise counsel—they realize personal accountability is an imperative if they are to consistently align with, and authentically *live* their values, mission, and vision."

"This Triple 'A' process: *Awareness – Alignment – Accountability*. How long does it take?" Josh asked.

Chuckling good-naturedly, George said, "A lifetime, Josh. The process takes a lifetime. Just when you think you arrive, the very act of arriving opens doors to new horizons of leadership development, and, for that reason, every values-based leader is a lifelong learner."

"I was afraid you might say that," Josh said with a smile.

• ● •

Josh heard the phone ring as the twins yelled in unison: "I'll get it!" After a brief scuffle, Ali emerged victorious and presented the phone to Josh: "Daddy, it's for you! It's Mr. Greenfield."

Josh greeted George with a warm "hello."

"Good evening," George replied, "I hope I am not interrupting anything."

"Not at all," Josh said.

"Josh, I won't detain you. I just want to extend an invitation. Tomorrow I have an appointment in Allentown with the CEO of

Finest Foods Emporium. For the past five years I've worked with Finest on a consulting basis. After you and I talked this afternoon, it occurred to me you might be interested in what their CEO has to say about Values-based Leadership, so I called and asked if you might join us. Would you be interested?"

"That would be great," Josh answered.

"Excellent. I'll drop by around nine and we can ride up together."

"Look forward to it. Thanks, George. See you in the morning."

Hanging up the phone, Josh wondered what revelations George had planned for the following day.

TWELVE

  ❝ The object of leadership
is the followers themselves. ❞

RICHARD PHILIPS

Josh and George were ushered into Lisa Caldera's unpretentious office. Rising from behind her desk, Lisa greeted the men warmly, with a broad smile and confident handshake: "It's good to see you, George," she said, "and this must be the friend you spoke about in such glowing terms. Welcome to Finest Foods Emporium, Josh."

"It's a pleasure to meet you, Lisa. What an incredible operation you have here! George and I came in through the supermarket entrance, and I want to tell you, it's the best laid-out and best merchandised store I've ever seen. And your employees were extremely friendly."

"Thank you, Josh," Lisa responded. "We're quite proud of our associates. It might sound cliché, but our people are the key to our success. Since our modest start fifty-two years ago we've grown to be perhaps one of the most progressive and most successful grocery chains in the country—and it's all due to the selfless contributions of our associates who have dedicated their talents and professional lives to our vision for Finest Foods."

"That's impressive," Josh said. "How did you manage to achieve such prominence?"

"Well, it's a long story. The thumbnail version is that I learned several secrets to organizational transformation—I discovered the power of Values-based Leadership," Lisa replied.

"I'd sure be interested in the longer version," Josh said.

> *I learned several secrets to organizational transformation—I discovered the power of Values-based Leadership.*

"Fine with me," George added, "I believe the time would be well spent."

"Have a seat then." Lisa gestured to a comfortable-looking couch.

Taking a seat adjacent to the coach, Lisa began: "My father, Victor Caldera, founded Finest Foods Emporium fifty-two years ago. Originally, Dad started out with my grandfather, Papa we called him, in a small produce business—actually a roadside stand. Dad used to spend all his free time touring grocery stores in the area and was under-whelmed with the appearance of the stores, the limited product offerings, and the apathetic attitude of employees.

"He began to dream about a store that would offer consumers exceptional service, a wide array of quality products and unparallel value. Dad believed customers wanted choices and value, and that they deserved respect, friendly service, and gratitude from the retail establishments they frequented. So, scraping together $25,000, he leased an abandoned department store in Allentown and began to create a new kind of food-shopping experience.

"Due to limited funds, standard merchandising fixtures were out of the question, so Dad built shelving using old crates in very creative ways. Before long, the interior of the store was transformed into a meticulously clean and well-organized 'old-world market' atmosphere.

"Meanwhile, Dad developed strong relationships with suppliers, especially those providing perishable goods like fish, meat, produce, and dairy products. You can imagine the suppliers' delight when he was willing to pay premium prices for their best goods.

"And, after hiring his first few employees, he spent an inordinate amount of time training the staff to be courteous, service oriented, and grateful for our customer's patronage. I can almost hear him now repeating the words: Service, Quality, Value, Respect, and Gratitude. In fact, he said them so often they've become our way of life here at Finest.

"As you might guess, many folks in Allentown responded well to the aesthetic shopping experience, exceptionally friendly and attentive clerks, and competitive pricing. Before long, the business was quite profitable due to the volume of goods that passed through our doors— despite the fact that Dad paid his suppliers and employees top dollar.

"You see, Dad believed wealth was not so much measured in financial gain, but in the value and service he provided for customers and in the way he gave employees opportunity to contribute toward something significant, in addition to providing for their families. As a result, our customer base grew rapidly and Dad had no problems attracting qualified and committed employees, so much so that during the next forty-plus years he managed to open a new store every other year in a triangular region bounded by Philadelphia, Harrisburg, and Scranton.

"Ironically, while his profit margins were lower than other grocery stores in the area, his revenues far exceeded competitors. Growth was steady and profitable during those first forty-seven years, and more recently we've virtually exploded, jumping from $630 million in revenue to $2.3 billion in just five years."

Josh was genuinely impressed. "Not bad for a privately held company that started from a $25,000 investment," he said. "But I've got to ask: How did the more recent extraordinary growth come about?"

Lisa's assistant, Diana, stepped into the room carrying file folders. "We grew dramatically," she offered, "because Lisa challenged us with a compelling and huge—almost audacious—vision of what we could become."

"Thank you, Diana," Lisa said, "actually, it's more than that…"

Again Diana broke in: "She's right, you know. It wasn't just vision, but the way she got everyone to buy into that vision. Lisa's a born leader and the world's greatest motivator!"

Smiling, Lisa turned to Diana: "Thank you for the compliment, but I'm afraid you're giving me more credit than I deserve."

"Facts are facts," she said as she placed the folders on Lisa's desk and left the room.

"As I was saying," Lisa repeated, "actually, it's more than that…"

Before she could say more, George interrupted: "Yes, it is more than that. Not only did Lisa provide a compelling vision, and not only did she inspire and motivate her associates, but she also led by example, subjugating her personal goals and ambitions to those of the company. If I may?" George asked looking to Lisa.

"Okay," Lisa replied, "but go easy, I'm already sufficiently embarrassed."

"What Lisa didn't tell you," George said to Josh, "is that five years ago, when her father passed away, Lisa was approached by a national food chain to purchase Finest Foods Emporium. The transaction would have brought her personal financial gain in the range of $350 million. However, the proposed acquirer had a reputation for poor customer service and was infamous for employee churn and low morale. Evaluating the offer, Lisa visited stores owned by the potential acquirer in three nearby states. What she discovered was a discount-store mentality that—while price competitive—was staffed by people grudgingly 'going through the motions' and 'punching the clock'…and dirty, almost ill-kept shopping environments."

"It was a difficult time for me," Lisa interjected. "Dad and I always worked closely together. His passing left a huge void in my life, both personally and professionally. I valued his insights and the stability he brought to our decision-making process. Finding myself suddenly at the helm of Finest, I felt isolated and alone, and the decision I faced seemed almost overwhelming. It was at that point that George entered the scene."

George continued: "My role was simply confidant and advisor to Lisa."

"But," Lisa insisted, "his counsel was instrumental to our growth. Without his guidance, we wouldn't be where we are today. You see, with Dad gone and such an important decision before me, I needed someone I could talk to…"

"What she needed," George interrupted, "was to be true to herself and to have confidence in herself."

"What I needed, was someone from the outside I could trust—someone who would help me do the right thing."

"You two have quite a mutual admiration society going," Josh observed. "Lisa, we both recognize and appreciate George's talents—so tell me, *how* did he help you do the right thing?"

"Well," Lisa said, "he asked me two very simple questions. George asked me…"

"…he asked you *what you are trying to do*, and *what it is about you that is standing in the way*," Josh interjected.

Laughing, Lisa said, "Exactly! Sounds to me like you've been spending a tad too much time with George!"

"I believe I have the floor," George said, hoping to direct attention away from himself and back to Lisa's story. "As I was saying, Lisa was struggling with a decision: Would she sell Finest Foods Emporium for enormous personal gain, or would she continue to own and operate the business? We were introduced by a mutual friend, and my role merely was to help Lisa determine what was best for her *and* for Finest Foods. Initially we spent a great amount of time discussing pros and cons of the deal. After several meetings, Lisa and I took a day away from the office. We focused on Lisa, what she believed about life, what her passions were, what she was interested in, what she valued—and yes, Josh, I did indeed ask her *what she was trying to do in life.*"

"Actually," Lisa cut in, "that question was the turning point in my decision. Reevaluating my passions, beliefs, and values, I began to realize the money I would receive from selling would leave me miserable if it meant I'd have to leave Finest. The company is my life's work; associates and customers are my family. What we created at Finest Foods makes *their* lives better. In short, if I walked away from those things I would, in effect, be walking away from my purpose in life. George's question also helped me understand why I even considered the deal in the first place. I realized I lacked a gripping vision to fuel my enthusiasm for the company.

"It's not that things were bad. I was confident in our mission: *Providing an exceptional shopping experience for our customers and an exceptional*

> *I realized I lacked a gripping vision to fuel my enthusiasm for the company.*

work experience for our people. Also, the values Dad modeled for so many years lived both on our walls and in our actions. Just ask any associate about company values and you'll hear: *Service; Quality; Value; Respect; Gratitude.* Despite the worthwhile mission and widely embraced values, something was missing…and that something was an energizing vision.

"So George walked me through a detailed, soul-searching process to create a compelling *preferred future* for Finest. He challenged me to connect with what was inside me and bring it to the surface. The result was a vision to replicate the Finest Foods Emporium model throughout the country, thereby offering an exceptional shopping experience to millions of customers and an exceptional work experience to tens of thousands of new associates. We even dared to dream of expansion into other parts of the world! Once I answered *what it was I was trying to do,* you may not be surprised that the very next day I called our potential acquirer to withdraw from negotiations."

"So it's kind of like a Cinderella story," Josh suggested. "You caught the vision, implemented it, and presto—today you're a $2.3 billion company."

"I wish it had been that easy," Lisa replied. "The vision was the easy part. The hard part was answering George's second question: *What was it about me that was standing in the way?*"

George reentered the conversation: "Self-awareness does not come easily, but Lisa was a willing and committed pupil. On the personal side, she had matters pretty well under control. I think perhaps her greatest challenges were in letting go of her weaknesses in order to focus on her strengths, and in creating the appropriate cultural environment."

"An accurate assessment," Lisa agreed. "It's true I felt the need to be a great leader and to that end I tried diligently to be perfect in every way, in every leadership competency. George helped me realize my efforts were in vain. He helped me understand the necessity of accepting my limitations, staffing to my weaknesses and focusing on my strengths. I learned to appreciate the fact that people don't want to follow me because I'm perfect,

> *People don't want to follow me because I'm perfect, but because I am genuine enough and authentic enough to admit that I am not perfect.*

but because I am genuine enough and authentic enough to admit that I am *not* perfect. That's how trust grows…and when trust grows among team members and employees, there's virtually no end to what can be accomplished.

"Other things George helped me realize were the need for alignment and accountability in the organization. Like any company, our executives were proud of their capabilities and the results they produced. And, our results were good—but they weren't great. And certainly the way we got things done wasn't going to enable performance necessary to achieve our new vision."

"What were some of the internal issues you faced?" Josh asked.

"Pretty much what leaders face in any organization," replied Lisa, "things like personal agendas, functional silos, and jockeying for position. Each member of the executive team had good intentions, but as is often the case, they tended to rely on their own perspectives and personal capabilities.

> *Each member of the executive team had good intentions, but as is often the case, they tended to rely on their own perspectives and personal capabilities.*

Each lobbied for position and power to influence the organization for what he or she thought was best. Additionally, we suffered from some accountability avoidance and even, to some extent, an entitlement mentality on the part of associates."

"So, Lisa, what did you do to address the issues? Or should I address the question to George?"

"Be my guest," Lisa said, nodding to George.

"Initially we interviewed the executive team and a cross section of associates," George began. "Next we conducted surveys to assess the corporate climate—to understand employee attitudes and beliefs. Assessing the data, we became aware of the current reality in the company. We learned about the collective passions of the executive team—and of the associates—and we began to understand the issues that created a gap between the company's current reality and its preferred future. Finally we developed a plan and initiated a program we called 'Performance Excellence.' Our goal was to improve execution in an operational context. The program started with the executive team—first in the area of self-awareness—then we focused on team awareness."

"Yes," Lisa added, "that was a critical step. We made a significant investment in time and money by conducting a leadership retreat in the Poconos. We met for three days, and George led us through an intense process to understand ourselves as individuals, to understand how we relate and engage as a team, and to understand how we interact with the organization. Frankly, there were some pretty edgy moments as we came to grips with our interpersonal interactions...and we had some stressful discussions around the topic of accountability.

"The first two days focused on awareness. We used George's 'PRO Development' assessment to identify each team member's 'Ideal Roles,' and then the 'Educational Keys' that would enable each individual to maximize his or her effectiveness in those roles. While I wouldn't describe the process as enjoyable, it was certainly engaging and productive.

"The last day of the retreat was mostly about alignment and execution. The team culminated the meeting by signing a pledge committing to alignment on the behaviors that would lead to the performance required to achieve our vision. Additionally, we set up a system for individual and team accountability.

"It was a tremendous experience, yet there were some pretty emotional moments. I remember one of our operations managers—a burly, sometimes course, rough-around-the-edges kind of guy—almost breaking down in tears when he realized how much the rest of the team valued his input and appreciated his expertise. And, there were numerous smaller breakthroughs, between individuals and in individual self-awareness. When we concluded the meeting, we had addressed—not solved, mind you—the major internal issues facing the organization. We also went away a more unified and supportive team. In my mind, the retreat set the stage for 'Performance Excellence' at Finest."

"The executive retreat created a platform for enrolling the organization," George said. "Each operations manager and functional head was charged with the responsibility of cascading the values, behavioral-norm expectations, and the new vision to their stores and departments. Over the course of several months, everyone at Finest clearly understood what they were trying to accomplish and what behaviors were expected to ensure appropriate execution. Throughout the company, supervisors met with their teams to articulate the vision. They shared behavioral expectations, addressing the issues previously identified by the executive team. Meanwhile, the executive team met on a regular basis to hold each other accountable for *living* the values and to develop appropriate strategies to achieve company goals."

"To address the question of strategies," Lisa added, "the executive team participated in a two-day 'Innovation Workshop' to challenge our status-quo way of thinking. We engaged in a series of exercises to spark our creative juices and to get us thinking outside the box. From those exercises came the strategies we launched to achieve the new vision."

George continued: "The new strategies were then cascaded throughout the organization with a challenge to every associate to determine how each individual could contribute to achieving the strategies. Associates were charged with the responsibility of creating personal action plans in support of the goals and objectives. As a result, associates became owners in the new vision."

"Which leads back to my statement at the beginning of our conversation: Our extraordinary growth is due entirely to the selfless contributions of our associates who committed their talents, creativity, and energy to achieving our vision for Finest Foods," Lisa summarized.

"With the story now told, perhaps we could break for lunch," suggested George.

Lisa agreed.

"Sounds good to me," Josh said.

THIRTEEN

❝ Culture eats strategy for lunch. ❞

RICHARD T. CLARK

Returning from lunch and a brief tour of the company's adjacent supermarket, Josh initiated the conversation. "It seems to me, Lisa, that earlier you were being unduly modest," he said. "From what you described, you played an instrumental role and exhibited incredible talent in leading Finest Foods to its current state."

"*Incredible* is certainly an overstatement," Lisa said. "In reality, part of my initial problem in leading Finest was the very fact that I *was* trying to exhibit outstanding leadership. I was trying to be 'Superleader.' I was trying to maximize *my* personal abilities to be *the* differentiating factor in our success.

"George helped me realize three critical truths: First, I cannot control outcomes on a wide scale, no matter how good or how talented I am. Influence outcomes, yes—control them, no. Second, George finally convinced me that organizational success doesn't depend solely on me… it's about *us* as a team…it's about *us* as an organization. And, third, George helped me understand that effective leadership is ultimately about the followers themselves; it's the followers, not the leaders, who actually execute strategies.

"Additionally, George helped me embrace the Values-based Leadership philosophy. Consequently, my personal goal over these past five years has been to internalize these truths, exemplifying

> *Organizational success doesn't depend solely on me…it's about us as a team… it's about us as an organization.*

them in my words and actions, while simultaneously instilling them in the hearts and minds of employees at every level of the company. And my goal for the company has been to create a culture that would benefit from the power of Values-based Leadership."

"Kind of a paradigm shift," Josh observed.

"It certainly was," Lisa replied, "and a major one at that. Imagine me trying to convince my executive team that what *they* bring to the party is inconsequential compared to what their followers bring, because it is the followers who actually execute the mission—who actually do the work.

> *Imagine me trying to convince my executive team that what they bring to the party is inconsequential compared to what their followers bring, because it is the followers who actually execute the mission.*

It takes a major dose of self-awareness and humility to swallow that idea.

"Leaders too often rely on our own capabilities, our business acumen, and our professional judgment to drive results. We try to have all the answers and solve problems rather than help our people find their own solutions. We task people to serve our needs and expectations rather than serve their needs and aspirations. Unwittingly we stifle the one critical resource necessary to achieve extraordinary corporate results: Willing, engaged, and motivated followers."

"Lisa took an interesting approach to convince the executive team of the validity of Values-based Leadership," George said. "Instead of simply mandating the philosophy, she started with the associates, asking them to create an 'Associates' Bill of Rights.' If I remember correctly, Lisa personally met with a fairly large cross-section of the company in four separate groups—one from each operating unit and one from corporate headquarters. During the meetings the groups drafted their respective versions of a 'Bill of Rights,' which Lisa then merged into one final document."

"Actually," Lisa added, "it was amazing how similar the lists were, and I was astonished at how closely the associates' lists aligned with the values George suggests as a staring point for Values-based Leaders."

"Could you show me a copy of the 'Associates' Bill of Rights'?" Josh asked.

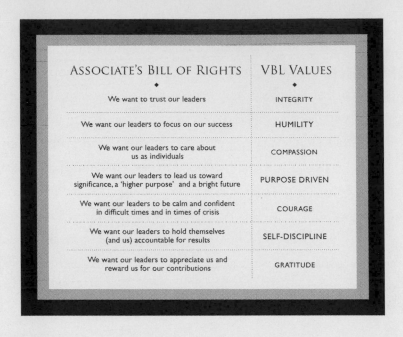

ASSOCIATE'S BILL OF RIGHTS	VBL VALUES
We want to trust our leaders	INTEGRITY
We want our leaders to focus on our success	HUMILITY
We want our leaders to care about us as individuals	COMPASSION
We want our leaders to lead us toward significance, a 'higher purpose' and a bright future	PURPOSE DRIVEN
We want our leaders to be calm and confident in difficult times and in times of crisis	COURAGE
We want our leaders to hold themselves (and us) accountable for results	SELF-DISCIPLINE
We want our leaders to appreciate us and reward us for our contributions	GRATITUDE

Pointing to a framed document on the wall, Lisa continued: "Interestingly, it was that exercise, and the resulting document, that enabled the executive team to acknowledge and embrace the tenets of Values-based Leadership. We realized if we treat our associates in the way they want to be treated, we could motivate them to performance excellence.

"And to appropriately motivate our people in this manner, we realized the necessity of aligning on, and holding ourselves accountable for *living* the values we espouse. Only then would our associates deliver expected results."

"It seems to me," Josh stated, "that motivation is one thing, but getting people—especially leaders—to work together as an executive team and to consistently exemplify expected behaviors, are altogether different matters. Once you established the 'Associates' Bill of Rights' and got the executive team's buy-in to VBL, how did you execute? I mean, how did the issues you mentioned actually get resolved?"

"A good question," interjected George. "The 'Bill of Rights' was a fine start, but it took quite a bit of follow-on work to create the corporate culture they needed. The fact is, every organization has a culture, and all boil down to this: *The way things are done around here.* With a haphazard approach to values, a corporate culture evolves with an 'every-man-for-himself' mentality, resulting in misalignment, lack of unity, stagnant business results, or worse, chaos. Ultimately, the result is sub-standard performance and a failure to execute well-intentioned strategies."

Resuming, Lisa said, "We realized we had to be intentional about creating a values-based culture, and, as you surmised, the work necessarily had to begin with the executive team. We needed to think and act as a team. If we couldn't work together effectively there was no way we could expect anything different from the rest of the organization. And we needed metrics by which to measure our effectiveness. George led us through a methodology to address these issues. First we conducted a 'Team Alignment Survey' and then met with the team to discuss the results."

Lisa went to her desk to retrieve a file, from which she produced a document titled: 'Issues Every Team Must Address.' "Here's a copy of the topics," she said, handing the paper to Josh.

Issues Every Team Must Address:

MISSION - to create purpose: Are we aligned on one clear mission and a common vision? Is our mission reflected in our goals and priorities?

VALUES - to determine behavior: Do we understand and embrace a set of shared values and does our behavior reflect those values?

TRUST - to establish unity: Is there a growing trust among and between members, or does lack of trust stand in the way of desired performance?

ALIGNMENT - to enable productivity: Are we committed to achieving corporate objectives or does ambition for individual success undermine team effectiveness?

ACCOUNTABILITY - to insure performance: Do we hold each other accountable for performance? Do we do what we say we are going to do? Do we deliver expected results?

"On the surface," Lisa continued, "the issues look straightforward and simple. However, we found the task more difficult than it appeared. For hours we talked about, argued, and debated the topics and how they pertained to our actual behavior and to how we operated as a team. Using the survey results as our baseline, we eventually agreed to actions that would improve our performance in each area. At the end of the day we secured alignment and commitment to an action plan… and, since then, we've revisited the questions on a quarterly basis.

"As a result, executive team members are more unified and mutually supportive of each other's success—we truly *are* a high-performance team. As our behavior and focus permeated the company, the resulting corporate culture reflects the executive team's behavior. I'm proud to say we now boast high-performance teams throughout the organization.

"In fact, the new culture enabled us to implement an organizational structure fairly unique in retail. We now delegate decision-making to the team level—small units that manage departments such as meats, produce, bakery, and etcetera. While store managers provide overall direction, a great deal of autonomy is given to respective teams. The teams decide what to stock and how to merchandise their products. They even have the final say in hiring decisions for their departments. Performance bonuses are paid out to teams—not to individuals. And we share financial information with the teams so that they will take ownership for the impact of their decisions.

"This cultural transformation was extremely important as we opened new stores and integrated acquisitions into our operations. Our mission, vision, and values unified us, sparking creativity and motivating associates to full engagement—engagement as owner-operators of Finest Foods Emporium."

"But the transformation you described wouldn't have occurred without the right kind of leadership," Josh insisted.

"Leadership is important," Lisa agreed. "The secret we discovered is that organizations will achieve superior and sustainable results when leaders address the foundation of behavior and performance—shared values."

"Here we go again with the *values* pitch," Josh interrupted with a smile.

Now George answered: "Yes Josh, I've said repeatedly that results of any type are predicated on values. Let me offer an example, focusing on one of Finest's corporate values: *service*. We find the model works like this: Associates *value* service, which leads to the *belief* that service is important and *Organizations will achieve superior and sustainable results when leaders address the foundation of behavior and performance—shared values.* makes a positive difference in working with each other, as well as with customers. This belief inspires associates to think about how they might actually demonstrate service, and it governs their *choices* about whether they serve the customer's wants and desires or their own—and whether they serve their fellow associates' needs or focus on their own preferences, desires, or ambitions. These choices result in observable and measurable *behaviors* that delight customers and support, affirm and motivate other associates. Collectively, the behaviors determine specific *performance*—in the case of Finest Foods, performance that develops trust and encourages innovation on the part of associates while creating loyal and satisfied customers—and ultimately result in astounding growth and significant return-on-investment."

"So," Lisa added, "we found it to be true: Values *do* govern behavior and behavior *does* determine performance—the kind of performance excellence we've experienced at Finest."

"I'd be a fool to argue with you, based on your results," Josh said, "and you seem convinced it's ultimately a matter of values being embraced and lived out."

There is one value of critical importance—and that value is humility.

"Absolutely convinced," Lisa replied. "Values are the key, and each value is important, but I believe there is one value of critical importance—and that value is humility."

"Unfortunately," George interjected, "I have an engagement I must attend to, and therefore must request we leave humility for future discussion. Lisa, this has been a delightful meeting, but with your permission, Josh and I should take our leave."

Reluctantly, Lisa and Josh acquiesced to George's request and the trio adjourned with sincere words of appreciation—and on Josh's part, with tremendous admiration for both Lisa and George.

On the ride back to Doylestown Josh was deep in thought. Finally, George asked: "What's on your mind, Josh?"

"I'm just trying to put the pieces together. Most of what you've been telling me about leadership makes perfect sense, even though it's contrary to my observation of so many leaders.

"What I'm struggling with is this notion of humility; and to be honest, I'm getting pretty frustrated. Do you realize, George, I've asked you about humility on several occasions and you've never once directly addressed my questions? It's almost like you hint at having some secret treasure, but you won't share it with me."

Silenced loomed in the car for the next few moments. Finally George spoke, measuring every word: "It's because…I can't."

"What do you mean?" Josh asked.

"I can't share the treasure—that is, humility—with you," George replied. "Please understand, Josh, it is not that I *will not*, it's simply that I *cannot*. The fact is I can't give away what I don't possess. In all honesty, it pains me to admit that I don't adequately possess humility. Josh, I avoid your questions because I struggle with the topic myself… despite the fact that I know deep in my heart that humility is the one indispensable ingredient to greatness."

"But George," Josh countered, "if humility is critical to leadership effectiveness and truly great achievement, shouldn't we explore ways to articulate, grasp, and live out the concept?"

"Yes," George replied with a chuckle, "I suppose we should. Are you willing to assist me in the endeavor, Josh?"

"Absolutely," Josh said.

FOURTEEN

> 6 6 I believe that the first test of
> a truly great man is his humility.
> I don't mean by humility, doubt of his power.
> But really great men have a curious feeling that
> the greatness is not of them, but through them. 9 9

JOHN RUSKIN

Several days later, comfortably seated in a quiet corner at Bucks' Beanery, George and Josh were immersed in the topic of humility. So far, the conversation had centered on research each had done on the subject in preparation for this discussion.

Continuing the dialogue, Josh remarked, "Actually, it amazes me how seldom humility is referenced in current best-selling books on leadership. With the notable exception of Jim Collins, the topic receives at best only honorable mention. How can something so critical to truly transformational leadership be virtually absent from current writings?"

"I found the same to be true," George said. "Very little is to be found on the topic of humility in modern texts on leadership. Perhaps it is because the topic is so misunderstood—perhaps it's because the value itself is so elusive. What I found interesting is that humility's antonym, pride, frequently is referenced…"

"Exactly," Josh interrupted. "And pride is usually mentioned as a good thing, almost as an end unto itself. Isn't it good to have pride? Isn't pride a positive attribute and motivator?"

"It probably depends on which aspect of pride you are referring to," George replied.

"What do you mean *which* aspect?" Josh asked.

"Well," George said, "there seem to be two distinct approaches to how one might address the concept of pride. The first is in the more positive sense, when one says he or she is proud of someone else. Usually what they mean is that they have admiration for, or positive feelings toward, that person. It's primarily a word used to suggest affirmation or acceptance of someone.

"When we consider pride as an antonym to humility, the meaning is altogether different, and, I believe, more accurate to the way pride is seen in most people. Let me flip through my notes…. Yes, here, Webster defines this aspect of pride as 'Inordinate self-esteem; an unreasonable conceit of one's own superiority in talents, beauty, wealth, accomplishments, rank, or elevation in office, which manifests itself in lofty airs, distance, reserve, and often in contempt of others.' This is arrogant and destructive pride. In fact, I'd go so far as to suggest that *this* pride is the primary cause of most dysfunction, 'turf battles,' and lack of alignment in organizations, as well as—on a larger scale—the cause of most injustice, societal ills, and suffering in the world today."

"That's a fairly damning statement," Josh suggested.

"Perhaps," George replied, "but let's examine the facts. When you read newspaper articles lamenting the escapades of corporate chieftains who have set themselves above the law, above acceptable standards of behavior—those who act as if their corporations

Pride is the primary cause of most dysfunction, 'turf battles,' and lack of alignment in organizations.

exist solely for their benefit, their prestige, their personal convenience, and their advancement—to what vice might you attribute their attitudes and actions?"

"I guess you could say, by definition, that pride causes them to act that way," Josh said.

"When business leaders pursue personal agendas, or when they seek to control others to get their own way, what might you say is the cause?"

"Again, pride is probably the motivation," Josh answered.

"What about when government officials faithlessly execute their duties in favor of their own recognition and reward, subjugating the common good for their own acclamation and advancement?" George asked.

"Pride again seems to be the culprit," Josh answered.

"Or, to bring the matter home, if you and Libby were to engage in heated debate over a difference of opinion, or if either of you steadfastly refused to relinquish control over a seemingly insignificant matter, what do you believe might be the primary cause?"

"Pride," Josh replied somewhat meekly, remembering a recent argument with Libby that he had been determined to win.

"Yes, Josh, the tragedy of pride is that pride is all about *Me*; it's about what *I* think; it's about what *I* want, and what *I* need. The prideful *Me* claims control, battles for command, wields authority to secure the best position, insists on compliance, intimidates to gain respect, and quite literally *expects* recognition and reward.

"Think about it, Josh; most disagreements among people—and even nations—arise from the clamoring of this narcissist *Me*. Pride results from the belief that I'm important enough, smart enough, capable enough, all-knowing enough, and deserving enough to take things into

> *The tragedy of pride is that pride is all about Me; it's about what I think; it's about what I want, and what I need.*

my own hands. Instead, our attitude should be the opposite—that it's not about *Me*, and there's no particular reason why *I* should get what *I* want—because the world does not revolve around me."

"And surely this negative impact of pride causes greater problems," Josh added. "Just think in terms of all that is wrong in the world today: People desperately searching for lives of purpose and meaning, the prevailing lack of compassion, lack of respect for individuals, the inequitable distribution of healthcare, widespread poverty, even starvation and famine—all seem to trace their source back to an unhealthy preoccupation with self, back to the issue of pride."

"An interesting thought," George affirmed, "tell me more."

"Well," Josh continued, "it seems to me that while leaders clearly impact the well-being of their organizations, they also profoundly impact the welfare of society as a whole. If a leader, even unwittingly, is fueled by pride and is therefore focused on *self*, inevitably he will fail to create an organizational culture that provides professional growth and a sense of significance on the part of followers, resulting in followers who merely exist to endure an environment devoid of hope and meaning. Followers will feel their contributions and efforts are all about the leader and won't be energized and engaged to achieve a higher purpose. The followers then return to their homes with an attitude of apathy, complacency, and dissatisfaction, which in turn infects their families and everyone with whom they come in contact. The repercussions are immense.

"Throughout my career I've too frequently observed self-focused leaders who fail to demonstrate sincere compassion and respect. Instead they create cultures where care and concern for other people are afterthoughts, and where there's a general lack of respect for people as individuals. This behavior extends to the way employees treat customers and suppliers and to the way people within the organization relate to coworkers with different points of view, different beliefs, and different cultures."

"I agree," George said. "And it then becomes clear how pride perpetuates the problems in society today. Pride drives leaders toward self-focus, causing them to concentrate their efforts on *what's in it for them*. As a result, those outside the leader's circle of self-interest have to make their own way. And when significant numbers of leaders adopt a pride-driven, me-first mentality, the result is a virtual sea of humanity left wanting for even the most basic human needs."

Josh interjected: "So, ultimately, the numerous ills that plague organizations, and even humanity as a whole, could be resolved if pride were eradicated. A transformation can occur if the destructive nature of pride is understood and the secret of humility embraced." Then, more solemnly, he added, "If humility is so unappreciated and misunderstood, is there any hope?"

"I honestly don't know," George replied. "What I do know is that the solution must start with me...with us. As someone once said, 'We must *be* the change we hope to see in the world.' Perhaps we

> *A transformation can occur if the destructive nature of pride is understood and the secret of humility embraced.*

should examine what we *do* understand about humility—what it is and what it isn't."

"Why focus on what it isn't?" Josh asked.

"Because," George responded, "if we can address misconceptions about humility, its positive attributes might be more readily embraced."

"Imagine asking a confident, self-sufficient, successful group of corporate leaders to define humility," Josh mused. "They'd probably say that humility has to do with false modesty, poor self-image, meekness, self-abasement, subjugation, humiliation, or even weakness. Obviously these traits are less than desirable."

"If leaders understand humility in relation to those attributes, is there any wonder why they'd avoid it at all costs?" George suggested.

"Probably not."

George continued: "And if leaders embrace these incorrect notions of humility, doesn't it stand to reason they'd naturally embrace the false positive of pride?"

"Yes, I can see where they would."

"So then," George elaborated, "given the destructive power of pride, it behooves us to understand and articulate the truth of humility, thereby providing a powerful and effective alternative to pride."

"What do you see as the power in humility?" Josh asked.

"Well, to begin," George answered, "it seems to me that humility is not false modesty. Rather, it is a full appreciation of our talents, coupled with the realization that our abilities are gifts...and that these gifts are given for the benefit of others. When others observe us using our talent

> *Humility is a full appreciation of our talents, coupled with the realization that our abilities are gifts...and that these gifts are given for the benefit of others.*

and ability for their benefit, they naturally respond with loyalty, contributing their best efforts for mutual achievement. Neither is humility poor self-image. Instead, humility illuminates counterfeit aspects of our lives so that we may live authentically to the full extent of our capabilities and effectiveness. True humility enables us to be comfortable with ourselves—to actually *be* ourselves."

"Continuing with your train of thought," Josh added, "I can see where humility is neither meekness nor weakness. Here, let me read the Hebrew definition of humility: 'The voluntary descent from rank, dignity or just claims; submission to others in granting requests or performing acts which strict justice does not require.' Given this definition of the word, humility is far from weakness…it indicates great strength and confidence on the part of the leader."

"And just think of the impact on others," offered George. "If a leader voluntarily steps aside from position, stature, and privilege, the result is not personal diminishment, but rather the opposite. He or she will receive increased respect and admiration as well as increased commitment and sacrifice from followers."

"So I guess it also stands to reason that humility is not involuntary subjugation or humiliation," Josh said. "If I appreciate my talents, live authentically, and voluntarily step aside for the sake of others, there is no subjugation or humiliation, because I made the choice from a position of strength—it was not imposed on me."

"Exactly," George concluded, "and—counter-intuitively—voluntary submission to humility results in increased leadership effectiveness and superior results. Ultimately humility enhances the quality of life and provides a platform to positively transform the human condition."

> *Voluntary submission to humility results in increased leadership effectiveness and superior results.*

"So," Josh concluded, "far from being diminishing or dehumanizing, sincere humility enhances individual worth."

"It does enhance a person's worth," George added, "because truly humble people are honest with themselves about their abilities, disposition, and motives. They're not ambitious for personal achievement, nor are they arrogant or boastful. They're genuinely caring and respectful of others, and they're serious in their commitment to better the lives of others. They persevere with a positive, uplifting attitude, even in the face of trials and hardships. They take responsibility for their performance and do not lay blame on others for their failures—and they genuinely appreciate and acknowledge the contributions of others."

"What you're suggesting," Josh deduced, "is that humility greatly impacts the other six values espoused by a values-based leader."

Affirming, George said, "Humility is the basis for the other values. Considering humility within the framework of VBL we see that *personal honesty* reflects the value of integrity. *Forsaking personal ambition* and *refusing arrogance* correspond to an aspect of humility. Demonstrating *care* and *respect* suggest compassion. Serious *commitment to selfless goals* reflects purpose-driven behavior. *Perseverance* in the face of hardships requires courage. Personal *responsibility* equates to accountability. And one who genuinely *appreciates others* demonstrates gratitude."

> *Humility, in its full definition, is the indispensable value of a values-based leader.*

"Therefore," Josh concluded, "humility, in its full definition, is the indispensable value of a values-based leader."

"Yes, Josh, it seems clear that values-based leaders must understand the critical importance of humility," George said. "They must understand humility is a vital truth that connects them to others.

It's what makes them approachable and allows dependency on others— a dependency that causes them to rely on others' abilities. Humility is the power of understanding that *I* can't, but *we* can. For the follower it actualizes the collective power in community. For the leader it is manifested in the power of the team—the power of *us*.

"While leaders may create strategy, strategy is executed at the base levels of an organization. It is humility that enables the leader to connect with the lowest level of an organization to ensure appropriate execution and achieve desired results. When all is said, it appears true that the one indispensable value of an effective leader is humility."

"And it seems to me," Josh commented, "that if it is genuine, humility is a slow and deliberate process that could take a lifetime."

"How true," George agreed, "how true indeed."

• ● •

That evening, when things had quieted in the McCall household, Josh wasn't sure where to start relating the day's events to Libby. He was enthusiastic about all he had learned, but he was a bit overwhelmed with the implications of all that learning.

He eventually began by recounting the discussion about humility, which naturally led to the topic of pride. In mid-sentence he stopped. After a brief pause, he said, "Libby, I need to apologize and ask your forgiveness."

"Forgiveness for what?" she gently asked.

"Do you remember the other day when we were arguing and I just wouldn't give in? Funny, but I don't even recall what we were arguing about…"

"It couldn't have been too important," interrupted Libby, "or you would remember the issue. Just let it go, honey, it's over and forgotten."

"Actually," Josh replied, "that is exactly my point: It wasn't important, but I just couldn't seem to let go. I wouldn't allow myself to lose. And that's why I'm apologizing; I need you to forgive me for trying to exert control—for allowing my pride to get in the way."

"It's over and forgotten," Libby repeated. Smiling, she continued, "And I forgive you. Josh, it really wasn't a big deal."

"Maybe the argument wasn't too significant, but I've come to realize pride—and all its negative connotations—is a very big deal," Josh said. "I'm beginning to realize what destructive power it holds. In fact, as I trace events of my career, I see I've made far too many decisions on the basis of pride."

"You're being too hard on yourself," Libby countered.

"Not really. I'm just being honest with myself. Think about it," Josh continued, "I left the army to pursue recognition and financial gain. I climbed the corporate ladder and was derailed on several occasions, due to my ambition. I failed at National Service Masters because I insisted on my own way. And, ultimately, I failed at consulting because I didn't understand the true essence of leadership—I didn't understand that leadership isn't about me. So, while I blamed every professional difficulty I've encountered on someone, or something else, the core issue is that I lacked the necessary humility to be truly effective."

"Is that what George told you?" Libby asked.

"No, George is far too gracious and kind to be that blunt," Josh replied. "But George has led me on a journey to discover the secret for myself—and for that I'm extremely grateful."

"So what do you do with it all…with your discovery?" prompted Libby.

"For now, I guess the only thing I *can* do is focus on being the kind of person I should be—one who focuses on others rather than on myself, and one who uses my talents and abilities for the sake of others," Josh answered.

"And what does that mean, practically, to your search for a job… one that you can enjoy and find fulfillment in?"

"Well, *practically*," Josh said with a grin as he reached to embrace Libby in a bear hug, "I don't know for sure. But I've come to realize the more I seek to serve and raise up others—the more I look for ways of bettering the world rather than myself—the more likely I am to land a job where I can truly make a difference and provide for you, my darling, in the way you deserve."

EPILOGUE

    " We are blind until we see
That in the human plan
Nothing is worth the making
If it does not make the man.

Why build these cities glorious
If man unbuilded goes?
In vain we build the world
Unless the builder grows. **"**

EDWIN MARKHAM

Josh watched out the window as the LAX tarmac faded from view. Gradually, as the jetliner gained altitude over the ocean, outlines of choppy waves were visible from the aircraft's small porthole. So far, everything had gone as planned since leaving his home in Doylestown earlier that morning. His flight to Los Angeles was on time, and Josh had no trouble making the connection to Tokyo.

Now, comfortably seated in business class, Josh settled in for the long flight. Closing his eyes, his thoughts drifted to events of recent years. *It's been an incredible journey*, Josh mused silently to himself, *far better than I deserve. Who would have thought, back when all this started, that I'd be winging my way over the Pacific to lecture on transformational leadership—especially after all the mistakes I've made. And now I have the privilege of speaking to an international audience of corporate executives. What an amazing opportunity!*

Indeed Josh's story was intriguing. He recalled his early rapid ascent of the corporate ladder and his even more rapid and devastating descent into prolonged unemployment. He remembered the self-focus that perpetually distracted him from focusing on organizational results, and he remembered the ego and ambition that fueled his lust for success while blinding him to the necessity of purpose. He remembered his unsuccessful attempt at buying a business, his inability to establish a consulting practice and, on the brink of despair, his chance encounter with George Greenfield—an encounter that led Josh on a journey of self-examination and reflection.

In many ways, Josh thought to himself, *I'm a very different person than when I first met George. Talk about imperfection! The lessons learned were hard, yet, looking back, quite necessary. Were it not for the difficulties I encountered, and the mentoring George provided, I never would have realized that I'm both the cause of my success and the cause of my failures.*

I needed to comprehend that, acting alone, my achievements are

> *I'm both the cause of my success and the cause of my failures.*

limited to what I personally can control and accomplish, but with motivated and empowered followers, there's virtually no end to what might be achieved.

And, I had to understand that I can only attract committed followers when I first address in myself the faults I so detest in others—faults such as pride, self-interest, ambition, greed, and insensitivity toward others. I may never be perfect, but at least I can strive to learn and grow.

Thanks to George, Josh did learn and grow, experiencing renewal, embracing purpose and committing himself to effective leadership in every aspect of his life. Impressed with his protégé's new self-awareness, his many talents, and his desire to make a difference in the lives of others, George invited Josh to join his leadership consulting practice.

That was six years ago.

Since then, Josh and George collaborated, working together with senior executives in organizations of all types—guiding and renewing them to embrace the power of Values-based Leadership.

Through their consulting efforts numerous organizations embraced the philosophy of VBL and consequently experienced extraordinary results. As reports of their work became public, VBL found broad-based acceptance, and the two men found themselves in demand by leaders seeking to transform their organizations. Ironically, having realized the accomplishments he sought so many years before, personal achievement was no longer Josh's motivation; he was far more interested in influencing others, in all walks of life, to have a positive impact in the world.

Now, forty thousand feet over the Pacific, Josh wondered what reception he would receive from the Asian leaders he was scheduled to address. Originally he believed the VBL philosophy would strike a chord with many business leaders in the United States. He had been surprised, yet pleased to learn that the concept of Values-based Leadership resonated with leaders around the world. In fact, based on correspondence they received, VBL transcended traditional barriers of culture and language: Leaders around the globe were connecting with the importance of values. As a result, both George and Josh received frequent invitations to speak to groups, large and small.

This current engagement, sponsored by an Asian Leadership Forum, positioned Josh to address an uncommon and somewhat unlikely assemblage of business leaders expected to attend from Japan, China, Singapore, Korea, Taiwan, and India. Josh marveled at the anticipated composition of the audience and was almost awestruck with the power of the VBL philosophy. Not only does Values-based Leadership provide

> *Values-based Leadership provides a cultural environment that profits from the power of diversity and capitalizes on differences among genders, creeds, and nationalities.*

the platform for extraordinary organizational results, but evidently it provides a cultural environment that profits from the power of diversity and capitalizes on differences among genders, creeds, and nationalities.

Considering these significant realizations, Josh was greatly humbled and somewhat overwhelmed by the task before him. He fervently hoped he would bring value to the audience and that the attendees would understand, appreciate, and embrace the message he was charged to deliver. Conscientiously he retrieved the portfolio containing notes from which he would compose his speech....

Speaker Notes
Asian Leadership Forum
Saturday, April 14

What Is Leadership?

Many definitions exist—probably in the hundreds. Leadership is about transformation.

Leadership is about change—it's about changing an organization *from* lifeless, lackluster, acceptance of the status quo *to* growth. Without growth any organization will die. Without growth any organism will die (our bodies begin to die once growth stops; so is it with an organization).

All organizations live or die by their leader: Living and thriving depend on the leader's effectiveness in creating vision for a preferred future *and* in establishing an appropriate values-driven culture that will deliver expected performance.

Leadership is about "being" (*who the leader is*) and "seeing" (*where the leader is going*). It's about enabling the execution necessary to drive organizational results.

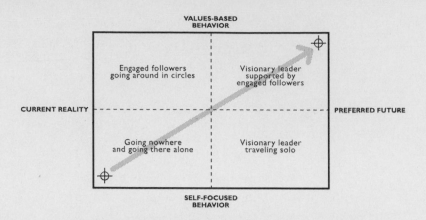

Leaders and their organizations best execute their mission and achieve superior results by first addressing the foundation of behavior and performance—personal and shared values.

Values govern behavior, and behavior determines performance. Values-based leaders effectively engage, motivate, and develop their followers, enabling transformational, sustainable change that leads to:

- effective execution
- productivity and efficiency
- innovation
- operational excellence
- outstanding results

The Leader's Role

Not to impose his or her will on others or on the organization,

   But instead ...

>   1. To act as a steward of the organization's mission, vision, values, and resources.

2. To creatively use his/her influence to motivate, energize, and facilitate growth in her/his followers.

Not to use power to achieve personal ambition,
   But instead …

1. To capitalize on *influence* in pursuit of organizational objectives.
2. To motivate performance and execution that matter to organizational results.

[Critical point] The leader, more than anyone else in the organization, must set himself/herself aside for the benefit and good of the followers.

Leadership Truths

I. Leadership is about the followers—it's not about me!
II. Effective leaders are purpose-driven [mission].
III. Vision is critical: to inspire, motivate and offer lives of significance.
IV. Character counts: Leaders must determine "who they are" [values]… before considering "what they are going to do" [vision].
V. Results matter: Execution drives results. Metrics are key to driving desired performance.
VI. It takes discipline and an intentional process to create a values-based organization (Awareness-Alignment-Accountability).
VII. Humility is the indispensable trait; humility precedes glory.

On Humility ...

The word *humility* stems from the root word *humus*; it suggests a connectedness with the earth and ultimately to a connectedness with all of earth's inhabitants.

Failing to see ourselves in this connectedness, we're not likely to be concerned by the injustices and inequalities that surround us *and* we'll turn a blind eye to troubled conditions that don't intrude on our welfare, or that don't threaten to disrupt our comfortable way of life. We will be content to pursue our own way, for our own benefit, and let it go at that.

When we lack intimate acquaintance with humility and an in-depth understanding of our connectedness we will too easily turn a blind eye to:
- poverty;
- wide-scale injustices;
- inequitable distribution of resources;
- unacceptable levels of healthcare;
- broken families;
- the unhappy state of millions of workers rambling aimlessly through life in search of significance and meaning.

Chinese proverb: "If we don't change our direction, we're likely to end up where we're headed."

If we engage in the practice of leadership to further our own goals and reputation, we inevitably will create an environment inviting our followers to do the same, thereby enabling self-focus to run rampant throughout our organizations. Self-focus does nothing to benefit positive organizational results; it serves merely to achieve personal results at the expense of the organization.

Leaders who wonder why dysfunction derails progress at every turn might do well to consider a personal change of direction, embracing humility as the catalyst for organizational health and achievement.

Humility as a value or in practice cannot stand alone; it must be exhibited in concert with other values to be authentic and effective. Humility without purpose is useless...

- apart from courage it is weak
- without integrity it is misguided
- in the absence of compassion it is not alluring
- without gratitude it is not genuine
- without accountability it is unsuccessful

Humility is essential and worth the effort because it enables an organizational culture capable of outstanding results.

Throughout history, leaders who exhibited *true* humility had the greatest positive impact—they made the greatest difference and achieved the most extraordinary results.

Examples ...

Mahatma Gandhi (India) peacefully led a fifth of humanity to independence, resulting in the world's largest democracy

Nelson Mandela (South Africa) broke the grip of apartheid

George Washington (United States) deserves much credit for establishing the United States as a nation, and for enabling civil and religious liberty

William Wilberforce (England) a reformer; largely responsible for abolishing England's slave trade

Jesus (the supreme example of humility) lived a life of love, service, and healing, leaving a legacy through committed followers who transformed human history.

Some might say humility comes from within, by our own determination or will, and some say it comes from divine inspiration. Either way, people experience humility through *who the leader is* and *what the leader does*—and that is the secret.

The Leader's Charge

- To understand and embrace humility.
- To pursue a life of purpose.
- To exhibit a life of character.
- To become dissatisfied with the status quo.
- To envision and articulate a preferred future.
- To create a performance culture and deliver results.
- To lead the way, serving at all times and at all costs.

Closing ...

Today I put before you the leader's charge. I encourage you to embrace the proven philosophy of Values-based Leadership and *be* the change you want to see in the world.

Transformational leadership seldom is an "all or nothing" proposition. Most leaders are neither great nor terrible—we are simply imperfect. Transformation occurs when we acknowledge our imperfection and set the growth process in motion.

Take heart: Values-based Leadership is not a destination, rather it is the path toward an ideal—and success is found in the journey. I fervently hope you will undertake the journey.

Josh completed reviewing his notes, setting them aside to consider meal options offered by the flight attendant. As he was served, Josh paused in gratitude for the wonderful life he had been given; for the amazing bond he enjoyed with Libby and their kids; for their enriching relationships with family, friends, associates, and people in the community; for friendship and mentoring he received from George; for his renewed direction and purpose; and for the opportunity to embrace, practice and share the secrets of truly transformational leadership—albeit imperfectly.

ANTE GLORIAM HUMILITAS

ACKNOWLEDGMENTS

66 The ideas I stand for are not my own. I
borrowed them from Socrates, I swiped
them from Chesterfield, I stole them from
Jesus. And if you don't like their ideas,
whose ideas would you rather use? 99

DALE CARNEGIE

As in any major endeavor, best results seldom are achieved alone; this
book is no different. In fact, were it not for the encouragement, support
and input of numerous individuals, *The Imperfect Leader* would not
have been written. My gratitude, appreciation and heartfelt thanks go
to the following:

• Denise, my wife, best friend, and partner, who constantly
encouraged me in this project, and who endured all the
emotion, frustration, and exhaustion that accompany such an
undertaking

• Gaines and Lauren (my son and daughter, of whom I am very proud) who not only encouraged me, but actually demonstrated sincere interest in the work

• The TAI Core Team, comprised of Tom Lombardi, Sue Green, and Rob Cook, who insisted I undertake this endeavor, who challenged and encouraged me to excellence, and who contributed valuable input, feedback, and advice

• Other members of the TAI Team who commit their talents to building a world-class organization. Many thanks to Warren Parry, Todd Hiestand, Jennifer Bacorn, Anne Israel, Selena Phelps, Gina Clear, and Carol Beers

• Wise counselors and advisors Don Evans, Bob Israel, Tom Christopoul, and George Schenk, who hold me accountable to the mission and purpose of TAI

• A wonderful PR and advertising guy, friend and valued advisor, Harry Hurst, who offered advice and gave me the title for this book

• A young and very talented designer, Zack Bryant, who developed the artwork for the cover and brought life to graphics and text within the manuscript

• A terrific editor and new friend, Jerry Gramckow

• My daughter Lauren, for her creativity in suggesting names for characters in the story

• Several dear friends: Rodger Adams, Adrian Pavitt, Len Tacconi, Rick Eimers, Matt Breitenberg, Rick Bremble, Kevin Carroll, and Barry Silverman who offered encouragement, insight and perspective as the book was written

- Clients from whose friendship, encouragement, and wise counsel I have benefited: Jerry Belle, Bob Feller, and Bill Bromage

- A great group of men who hold me accountable to my faith and who frequently remember me in prayer. Humble thanks to my son, Gaines; my brothers, Gregory and Jonathan; and my friends Wes Coddington, Hank Zuczek, Cam Garven, Mike Raymond; and again to Adrian Pavitt and Rodger Adams

- A mentor and role model of humility, George Gallup, Jr.

- My mother, Roberta Taylor, who demonstrated love and intense curiosity. And yes, Mom, it's finally finished

- My in-laws, Rodgers and Jerry Gaines, who manage to trust me with their daughter and always believe In me, no matter what.

BIBLIOGRAPHY

Bennis, Warren and Nanus, Burt, *Leaders: The Strategies for Taking Charge* (New York, NY: Harper & Row Publishers, Inc., 1985).

Bennis, Warren, "The Leadership Advantage" Leader to Leader, #12 Spring 1999. http://www.pfdf.org/leaderbooks/L2L/spring99/bennis.html.

Collins, Jim, *Good to Great* (United States of America: HarperCollins Publishers, 2001).

Kotter, John and Heskett, James, *Corporate Culture and Performance* (New York, NY: The Free Press, A Division of McMillan, Inc., 1992).

PRO Development™, TAI Incorporated, www.taiinc.com.

Strong's Exhaustive Concordance, 1890.

Webster's Dictionary of American English, 1828.

ABOUT THE AUTHOR

Davis Taylor leads TAI Incorporated, a consulting firm that specializes in Values-based Leadership. Prior to founding TAI, Davis had twenty-three years practical leadership experience in organizations ranging from a high-tech start-up company to Fortune 50 corporations. He and his family currently reside in Bucks County, Pennsylvania. He may be reached at davis.taylor@taiinc.com.

13565152R00104

Made in the USA
Lexington, KY
09 February 2012